SALESPERSON
TO SUPERHERO

SALESPERSON TO SUPERHERO

UNLEASH THE SUPERPOWER
OF RELATIONSHIPS

—᙮᙮᙮—

Ron Adams

Salesperson to Superhero:
Unleash the Superpower of Relationships

© 2017 Ron Adams

ISBN 0974060232
ISBN 13: 9780974060231

Chilidog Press, Loveland, Ohio

For information, contact the author:
Ron Adams
Bastion REALTORS®
384 Bridge Street
Loveland, Ohio 45140
Office Phone: 513-683-1777
Email: Ron@BastionRealtors.com
Website: www.BastionREALTORS.com

Published by:
Chilidog Press LLC
Loveland, OH
www.chilidogpress.com

Cover:
SaitaStudio
Suntmalu@gmail.com

CONTENTS

Introduction · ix

FIND YOUR WHY

    Episode 1:   Spider-Man makes *The Choice* · · · · · · · · · · · · 1

    Episode 2:   Superman exposes the *Sales Culture* · · · · · · · · 9

    Episode 3:   Daredevil experiences *The Awakening* · · · · · 30

    Episode 4:   Green Arrow's *Purpose Driven Business* · · · · 39

    Episode 5:   Captain America shows *Self-Awareness* · · · · · · 48

TELL YOUR STORY

    Episode 6:   Captain Marvel and *The Power of Words* · · · · 57

    Episode 7:   Batman deploys *Media* · · · · · · · · · · · · · · · 70

    Episode 8:   Justice League forms a *Tribe* · · · · · · · · · · · · 79

EXECUTE YOUR MISSION

    Episode 9:   Wonder Woman has a *Great Product* · · · · · · · 90

    Episode 10: Boy Wonder finds *Self-Development* · · · · 98

    Episode 11: Iron Man takes *Action* · · · · · · · · · · · · · · · 108

Worksheets · 123

Bastion Beliefs · 139

Book Reviews · 143

Acknowledgments · 155

About the Author · 161

Dedicated to my wife Theresa,
unselfish in all of her ways.

INTRODUCTION

—◦◦◦—

THE DATE IS OCTOBER 13, 1992. Admiral James Stockdale, the vice-presidential running mate of Independent presidential candidate Ross Perot, is preparing to debate Republican Dan Quayle and Democrat Al Gore in their only televised debate.

Not a politician, but a retired Admiral who won a Medal of Honor for heroism as a former prisoner of war during the Vietnam War, Admiral Stockdale is not in his natural element. This career military man is in an arena that is foreign to him, doing linguistic battle with two polished politicians.

Al Gore and Dan Quayle have finished their opening remarks and the world turns its attention to the Admiral. Hands shaking, he nervously stammers one of the most memorable opening remarks in debate history: "Who am I? What am I doing here?"

The audience erupts with laughter from this refreshingly simple non-politician. The "Stockdale question" becomes a punchline. But his questions are asked by all of us at some point in our lives.

Like Admiral Stockdale, we all want answers.

Unhappy with my life and my business, I decided to explore these important questions. Who am I? What am I doing here?

This book is the result.

As an 8-year-old boy I was enamored with comic books. My step dad had a stack that was almost as tall as me. I would read these comics with great anticipation and escape into a world where superheroes would defend the innocent in epic battles against villains who are intent on world domination.

I would read every word in these comics and carefully take in each illustration. Once the story and illustrations were exhausted I would read all the advertisements.

One advertisement that captured my imagination read: "Make Money, Get Prizes." Excited about the idea of making money and winning prizes, I decided to clip the coupon and send it in.

Selling seeds for the American Seed Company was my introduction to entrepreneurism. That's right, 8 years old.

Going door-to-door, I learned to prospect, present a sales pitch, get rejected, knock on another door, finally make a sale, deliver the product, collect the money and send it in. You know, run a business.

Years later, as an adult figuring out life, I stumbled on truths that have changed my business, my view on the meaning of life, and how I can best navigate this adventure.

This book is not only for real estate agents, but for all small business owners, salespersons, and anyone who is looking to improve.

This book is my invitation to you. An invitation to join me as we attempt to answer these questions together. We will look deeper into the purpose of our lives and the purpose of our business. We will explore how our business lives and our personal lives can successfully merge into one. One life. Authentic. No apologies. No hedging.

Together, we will explore the subject of self-awareness and implement a self-audit to help you discover what your natural point of aim is, what your strengths are, and identify your weaknesses. This audit will help answer the question, "Who am I?"—which in turn will help satisfy the question, "What am I doing here?"

Simon Sinek, the author of *Start With Why*, would call this your "*Why.*" This becomes the core of who you are as a person, and ultimately the driving force for your business.

Once we know our "*Why,*" we can go about building our business and living our lives with congruency. The question becomes: "How?" How do we do it? What are the options?

Also, we will discuss the two types of cultures in business: The sales culture and the relationship culture.

Doing business based on relationships is a more satisfying and sustainable model.

But how are relationships built?

Through stories.

We will explore how to tell your story and how to build relationships through your story that will contribute to your "*Why*," build your brand, and create a business consistent with your beliefs.

We will look at ways to build your audience with the current tools and technology available. In the process, we will explore the power of the written word, the psychology of influence and how to create a business "religion."

Once you understand the importance of your story, your message and your business religion, you will have to execute an action plan. I include chapters that will show you how to achieve real results, such as becoming a media company, distributing the message, and building a great product with a documented approach. In Episode 3 I also discuss how to get into the right mindset, through self-development, using what I call the "Five Capitals." And finally, I have a chapter on action—the foundation to all success.

Throughout the book I will share with you my story. The story of a desperately lonely, very poor, yet hopeful 8-year-old who fell in love with business after reading ads in the back of a comic book. It's the story of a kid raised in chaos who found peace and meaning on his journey to becoming an entrepreneur.

When an 8-year-old sees a superhero do the impossible, suddenly everything seems possible—even running a business before I entered fourth grade.

Comic-book heroes become superheroes because they overcome adversity. There comes a time when the character has to make a decision whether or not to fight.

Similarly, real estate, and business in general, is an epic battle. However, the enemy is not your competition. No, the real enemy is the face in the mirror. You know, the one who is consumed with self-doubt, anxiety, and stress.

The war within, the battle for your mind, is in full effect. Every. Single. Day.

Your enemy stands between you and success that changes lives. The business you create provides for your family, funds your government, contributes to your church, and helps local charities.

Yes, my friend, this battle is worth fighting. Your family and your community are counting on you.

I wrote this book so that you might be made aware of this battle. Today you may feel defeated. But I want to encourage you to win the battle, and in the process become a superhero.

It is my hope that you will read this book, hear my story, learn from my mistakes, and resolve to join the fight.

"Who am I?"

"Why am I here?"

These are the great questions in life. We all want answers.

Let's get started.

SPIDER-MAN MAKES THE CHOICE

—ɯɯ—

With great power comes great responsibility

"Not everyone is meant to make a difference. But for me, the choice to lead an ordinary life is no longer an option."

-- *PETER PARKER*

YOU'VE PROBABLY SEEN THE MOVIES, but do you know the real story of Spider-Man?

Peter Parker was orphaned as a child when his parents died in a plane crash overseas. An only child, he was raised by his elderly aunt and uncle. Peter was academically gifted and applied his talents with passion in his favorite subject, science. His life changed dramatically at a science fair at the age of 15 when Peter was bitten by a spider that was irradiated by a particle beam. The bite empowered him with many of the abilities of the spider. In an instant, he had strength, agility, and balance that was superhuman. Incredibly, he now had the power to cling to any surface, to crawl up walls and cling to the ceiling. But he also had a hyper sensitivity to impending danger, a sixth sense.

Peter deployed these new skillsets to make extra money. Disguised, he defeated wrestler Crusher Hogan in the ring, and with the accompanying fame he decided to put on a television special highlighting his powers. He called himself Spider-Man. In the TV special, he showcased his newly found athletic prowess and ability to walk up walls and cling to ceilings.

After the first TV special ended, he encountered a burglar whom he could have easily apprehended, but allowed the man to run past him and escape. Not one to get involved, and maybe still a little shy, he did not see the need to intervene.

Later, Peter returned home to find his beloved Uncle Ben had been shot and killed. In a rage, he set out to find the killer. When he caught up to the burglar as Spider-Man, in an abandoned warehouse, he realized to his horror that it was the same man he encountered and let go a few days earlier. Consumed with guilt, Spider-Man realized that with great power comes great responsibility, just as his Uncle had once said.

He vowed, "Never again." Being passive was no longer a choice. He would deploy his superpower to do good in the world, so that future "Uncle Ben's" would not pay the price.

And so it is with me.

I'm not Spider-Man. But I, too, have discovered a superpower, and have learned that with great power comes great responsibility. Accordingly, I believe it is my duty to share with you this power, so that you don't go down the same road that I have traveled. So that you can avoid the mistakes I've made and the pain I have experienced.

This superpower will unleash your business like nothing you have tried before. This superpower has sustainability, predictability. This superpower will lead you to self-discovery, and that will lead to a purpose-driven business. This superpower will change the world you live in, and it will change you and your business along the way.

This superpower is ***relationships.***

DEFINITION OF RELATIONSHIPS

In your life, you probably only have one best friend. Because of time and attention limitations, you can't possibly have hundreds of best friends or really close relationships. For the purpose of this book, let's agree that the relationships we are discussing are not your family or your very close friends. Those folks deserve a very special place in our lives, and also deserve most of our time and attention. Instead, the relationships we will discuss are the 150 to 200 people with whom you regularly come into contact.

In the real estate community, they call it your SOI or "Sphere of Influence." You know, your doctor, neighbor, or pastor at your church.

These relationships, when properly developed, become the foundation of a very healthy real estate practice.

My goal with this book is to guide you toward building these relationships while at the same time avoiding short-term transactional thinking, otherwise known as "the sales mindset."

THE CHOICE

Spider-Man had to make a choice—continue with his normal life or take action and become a crime fighter. Likewise, you, my friend, have a choice. It is unavoidable. You must declare now your allegiance. Do you build your business on the foundation of a sales mindset—transactional, short-term, focused on the sale? Or do you instead build on a foundation of relationships? Do you tap into the relationship mindset—a superpower?

You see, real estate is now an industry that has a negative reputation. Before someone ever meets a real estate agent, they already have a negative impression. Most people view real estate agents the way they see politicians, lawyers, and telemarketers. Why? How did this come to be?

In today's real estate environment, the agents who make the most sales, the large real estate sales teams, have turned the business into a giant call center with telemarketers in every cubicle. First they try cold calling you, and if that doesn't work they show up at your front door unannounced looking for their next score. No longer do they offer a superior service, but in order to grow they are now most interested in "leads." Not clients, but names, phone numbers, and email addresses. Where is the next sale? How do I get more leads? This is the sales mindset and it is the antithesis of the relationship mindset.

How did it get to this point? How is it that real people with real lives and families and careers are now just "leads?" How did the sales culture take over this industry and so many others?

We'll discuss this question in greater detail in Episode 2, but first let's take a look at how I got here. Let's talk about my transition into the real estate industry.

MY STORY

It was a crisp autumn morning. Jay and I had our usual breakfast appointment at Bob Evans Restaurant to discuss basketball. My 8-year-old daughter Krista had just joined the basketball team. Coach Jay and I would get together and discuss our practice schedule and game plans for the upcoming week.

But basketball was just an excuse. Jay and I really didn't need to meet to discuss the practice or plans for the upcoming week. Truth is, we just enjoyed each other's company. Having daughters the same age and our shared interest in basketball brought us together. We connected instantly. We had an unspoken understanding: He would start speaking, and I would understand exactly where he was going. I could even finish his sentences. To this day, I affectionately call him "Coach," which is to me the most fitting term.

As I entered the restaurant I could see he already had a table. He waved me over, and before I sat down I noticed he was taking in my slacks and sports coat with a confused look on his face. "Wow, you look professional," he said. And then he made a statement that would change the trajectory of my life. "It just occurred to me, Ron. I'll bet you would be a great real estate agent."

Although I knew Jay was a real estate broker I had not considered becoming an agent. My wife and I had bought and sold several houses over the years, but I really didn't know the first thing about real estate. At the time, I was working for Pella Windows as a sales representative. My job was to call on builders and architects to engage them, build a network and promote our doors and windows. I liked my job, but I didn't *love* my job.

I don't remember what else we discussed that morning but I couldn't get Jay's voice out of my head: "I'll bet you would be a great real estate agent."

You see, I am an entrepreneur. When I daydream, I dream about owning multiple businesses, traveling from place to place to check on my enterprises. In my dreams I hire great people, set up a dazzling website, create a new product and solve problems. I create happy customers and build a community of teammates who want to accomplish something big. My dream is to build something new and, through my business, make the world a better place. Silly, perhaps, but true.

MY EARLY CAREER

My job before selling doors and windows was as a manager for Payless Cashways, a lumberyard and home center chain. Think Home Depot, but a little smaller with a seven-acre lumberyard around back.

It was the summer of 1988 when I was accepted into the Payless Cashways "management training program." Payless trained me in every facet of the business, and then the promotions began. I was a department manager, showroom manager, lumberyard manager, operations manager, and finally a commercial sales manager—all within the same company. To a creative type, a purebred entrepreneur, it was the perfect education. I learned systems, but had the ability to engage creative problem solving and to learn people skills.

With each new responsibility, Payless gave me an opportunity to deploy my creative skills to take business that was underperforming and turn it around.

I truly loved working for that company and learned so much about customers, employees, and growing a business.

In 1997 Payless began having financial difficulty as the competition from Home Depot, Lowe's, Builders Square, and Home Quarters intensified. Simultaneously, a Wall Street investor began buying up Payless stock. To avoid the breakup of the company, senior management decided to borrow money to protect against losing control. This leveraged buyout caused a very high debt burden, which caused cash flow issues and inventory problems.

Because of the lack of inventory, customers, especially contractors, began to complain, and as a manager I heard the feedback daily. These regular phone calls and interactions made me realize that the company was in serious trouble. As I addressed the inventory issues it became clear the company was failing to pay its suppliers.

The valuable lesson for me during this time was that your customers are your best market research. If you want to know what decision to make for your business, just ask your customers. And more importantly, watch what your customers are doing—something I still practice in my businesses today.

I decided to leave Payless in the fall of 1997. The entrepreneur in me wanted to get into direct sales and have unlimited income potential. I found a company that needed a manager to start up their door and window division for their already successful lumber business.

As a manager for Paxton Lumber, I had the opportunity to, yet again, practice as an entrepreneur within an organization as I grew their door and window business. While learning my craft I was continually recruited by other window manufacturers to sell their products. In the winter of 2000 I decided to leave Paxton for Pella Windows to do the same job.

So there I was at Bob Evans with Jay. My entrepreneurial instincts and sales career had led me to this moment with my daughter's basketball coach and his observation: "I'll bet you'd be a great real estate agent."

As I thought about what Jay said I wondered: Could real estate be a way for me to start my own business, and stop selling for other people? Could I take that path to create my own future, deploy my skills and make my own mark?

The more I thought about it, the more it excited me. I could start by selling real estate part-time and then, over time, do it full time. After I had established myself I could get into real estate investing, which I had wanted to do for some time. Then I could open my own lumberyard— another dream of mine. Yes, this could be the start of something BIG!

Full of enthusiasm and hope, I started into my new venture. I took my classes, passed the exam, and I was licensed by the State of Ohio as a real estate agent.

And then I was introduced to the "Sales Mindset."

SUPERMAN EXPOSES THE SALES CULTURE

—⁂—

What is your kryptonite?

"I've got a bulletin for you, folks. I am no Superman.
I realize that now, but I didn't always."

-- CHUCK NORRIS

JOR-EL WAS A RENOWNED SCIENTIST who discovered a great truth—a fantastic, horrible, terrifying truth. His research discovered that his planet was doomed. It was only a matter of time. His calculations led him to the conclusion that his planet would soon self-destruct.

His fellow scientists dismissed the predictions and labeled him as a madman. Jor-El's belief's cost him his friends, his peers, and his reputation as a scientist.

Determined to save his wife Lara and his newborn son Kal, Jor-El built a ship designed to save his family from the imminent destruction.

While preparing the ship, his home and the planet Krypton began to disintegrate. He was too late. He only had enough time to save his infant son on the journey—alone. As the vessel was launched and sped through space, Krypton exploded and took the lives of Kal's parents.

Ultimately the ship landed in a field in Kansas where the boy was found, alive.

He was found by Jonathon and Martha Kent, a farming family. They took in Kal and decided to raise him as their own.

Renamed "Clark Kent," he grew as the family surrounded him with love and the necessities of life. However, the Kent's new adopted child showed amazing physical strength and abilities. They encouraged him to use these gifts for the good of mankind.

After Clark's parents passed away, he moved to Metropolis where he became a journalist working for the local newspaper, *The Daily Planet*.

As Superman, Clark Kent protected the citizens of Metropolis and fought for truth, justice, and the American way.

As everyone knows, Superman is faster than a speeding bullet, more powerful than a locomotive and leaps tall buildings at a single bound. Unless there's even a grain of Green Kryptonite around. Every superhero has a weakness, a "vulnerability." Green Kryptonite makes Superman slow and weak because it comes from his own Planet Krypton, which exploded right after his parents launched him off to earth in his survival capsule.

Green Kryptonite makes Superman powerless, weak and trapped because it contains the pure essence of mistakes from his past.

If you are feeling powerless, weak and trapped, you may be suffering from your own Green Kryptonite the same way I was. By telling my own story, I hope I can help you figure out what is holding you back from success and happiness.

"Sales Mindset" is my personal Green Kryptonite—created and fostered by the sales culture in the real estate industry. This culture is made up of real estate brokers, trainers, and coaches who litter the industry with their phone scripts, sales techniques, and motivational speeches. Focused mostly on getting leads and transactions, this type of training emphasizes transactional thinking and short-term behaviors.

Let's review my experiences with this sales culture and explore how, just like Superman, you can be seduced into this most dangerous of mindsets.

MY EARLY REAL ESTATE CAREER

My first year in the real estate business focused mainly on getting licensed, learning how to write contracts and understanding the real estate transaction process. Interesting subjects, but not terribly exciting.

I wondered, "What's next? How do I grow my business?" I asked my broker and fellow sales agents. And that was my introduction to the sales mindset, otherwise known as the sales culture.

The first thing you must do, they taught me, is to let everyone know you are in real estate. Make a list of everyone you know. This is called your Sphere of Influence, or "SOI." Once your list is made, start calling.

Sweet. That sounds good. "So, what do I say?" I asked.

They said, "Tell them you have started this new venture and you're really excited about it, and you need their help. Follow up by sending them a handwritten thank-you card along with your business card. Once you have established contact with them, put them into your database so you can follow up with them regularly."

Alright, now we're getting somewhere. "What's next?"

"Now you must stay in touch with them regularly so that when they need real estate advice, you will be 'top of mind.'"

Top of mind?

Yes, most people are not looking to buy or sell real estate. The sales cycle (time between transactions) is on average seven to ten years.

Seven to ten years? How do I stay in touch for that long? Won't I go broke by then? I can't wait seven years to make a sale!

No, you are not necessarily waiting for the people in your database to have a need. What you are after is a referral. You see, most people have their own SOI, folks they can influence. And depending on whom you ask, that number is about 150 to 200 people.

While you continue to contact your Sphere of Influence, once a month preferably, there are other ways to grow your database. The larger your database, the better chance you will have of scoring a transaction.

Oh. So not only do I create a database of people I know, but I also add people to my list each month as I meet new people?

Yes.

For the first few months I was busy building my list, contacting my SOI, sending business cards and thank-you notes. Once I had exhausted the list of folks I knew and picked up a few clients along the way, I had to make a difficult decision. How do I stay in touch with these folks on my list?

The experts said I should call, email or send something of value every month.

That was my first marketing decision. I chose to send something of value. Direct mail. I hired an outside vendor, the first of many. They had the most sensible product, a postcard with a healthy recipe. It was valuable, could be saved and was a way to stay in touch.

But, it wasn't enough. Although the monthly mailings had the best return on investment, they did not supply enough reliable business to be sustainable.

Now it was time to get real. Time to take action.

So down the rabbit hole I went, chasing… the SALES MINDSET!

And so it began. The treadmill. Not just chasing, but chasing strangers. People who don't know me, probably don't like me, and don't trust me.

LISTINGS FUEL GROWTH

The key to success in real estate, the experts said, is to attain *listings*.

Listings are houses for sale in which you and your broker have a listing agreement with the seller. The idea is to list at least one house per month. This puts your sign in the yard, promotes your business, and most importantly creates incoming phone inquiries about the property. These calls are potential buyers interested in the house. These same prospects become leads. The listing becomes the bait to attract more fish, or the honey to attract more bees, or whatever metaphor you would like to use. Bottom line: listings are the fuel to grow your business.

How do you get listings? The Sales Mindset had the answer.

FOR SALE BY OWNERS, 'EXPIREDS,' AND OPEN HOUSES

For Sale By Owners, otherwise known as FSBOs ("fizbos"), are listings by homeowners who would like to sell their home without a real estate broker. It is perfectly legal. The goal for the homeowner is to save money. Instead of paying 6 percent or 7 percent of the sales price to a real estate broker, they can sell the property and keep the commissions. However, only about 13 percent actually sell the home on their own. In the end, most list their home with a broker.

FSBOs are easy to find and easy to contact. They put a sign in the front of their house with a number to call. For a salesperson, that's low-hanging fruit.

You call the FSBO owner, develop a rapport, and convince the home-owner to list the home with you. Because of my sales mindset, this made total sense to me. I thought: "I am a salesperson. This is a potential sale. Let's sell this homeowner on the idea that I am the best person for the job."

I set out to make a list of these folks and stay in touch with them, hoping to convert them to a listing. If unsuccessful initially, I would add them to my database and stay in contact.

Next were "Expireds"—homeowners who have tried to sell their home through a broker but have failed. Their listing contract has run out and they are no longer obligated to their broker. They still want to sell their home, but in most cases they are unhappy with the "Expired" broker and won't renew. That's where I could step in: Solicit the seller, build rapport, and ultimately convince the homeowner to list the home with me.

Like FSBOs, "Expireds" are strangers who have no history with you as the agent. Yet still, low-hanging fruit.

Finally, let's talk about Open Houses. This strategy has long been accepted in the real estate business. Agents promote this to their sellers as a way to market their property. However, real estate insiders know the true intent is something else altogether.

The goal of an Open House public showing is really to meet potential buyers. Interested neighbors, fellow agents, and potential buyers will show up—new "prospects" and "leads." All those names, numbers, and emails can be added to your SOI and your mailing list, for regular contacts and potential new business.

Even though I didn't have listings of my own early in my career, I would hold Open Houses for some of my fellow agents and for a builder friend who had a market home he was trying to sell. As I met folks at an Open House I would have them sign in. If they hesitate, my peers told me, just tell them the owner wants the information for security reasons. Hmmm. Well, okay. Seems a little deceptive, but it's just business.

Sales mindset.

So far, I had added all of our friends and family to the list, all the folks I met at Open Houses, people we recently met at church, even new friends from the coffee shop. All strangers, all unsure of who I was, wondering if I was trustworthy.

My list of FSBOs and Expireds grew, along with my Open House contacts and my sphere of influence. Now what?

My fellow agents would advise me to contact everyone on the list once a month to build a relationship and stay top of mind. "While you have them on the phone, you can ask if they know anyone who is buying or selling real estate. You know, ask for the sale. You're in sales, you know!"

Okay, let me get this straight. I am in sales, therefore I am a salesman, so act like one?

Awesome, I thought, this should be easy for me. You see, my background was sales. My latest job at the time was selling doors and windows, but before that I managed a fourteen-person sales team for a Fortune 500 company for more than eight years. We didn't sell anything glamorous, just lumber and building materials, but selling was something I had been doing almost my entire life.

So I created a thirteen-week call planner, borrowed from my days in the lumberyard. There are thirteen weeks in a quarter, so I determined to call each person on my Sphere of Influence list at least three times each quarter. As I worked my way through the list, I could remind them that I was in real estate and ask for referrals.

Ring. Ring. Ring.

"Hi Mom."

"Hi Ronnie." (People who are close to me call me Ronnie... secretly I love this.)

"Mom, you know recently I received my real estate license. I was just calling to see if you knew anyone who was buying or selling real estate?"

"No hon', but I'll keep you in mind if I do."

"Okay, thanks, Mom, gotta go…"

"But, wait, how are the kids doing?"

"They're great, Mom, I'll catch up with you later. Love you."

Click.

I can imagine her reaction on the other end of the phone: a bewildered look as she held the receiver, looked at it, and wondered, "What in the world just happened?"

But she didn't understand: Even my mom was a lead. Sales mindset.

I was excited. I had a system. If I made only five or ten calls a day, I was sure to get some referrals.

Real estate is a "contact" sport, they say. (So clever, get it? Contact sport.) The more contacts you make, the more opportunities you create, the more leads you generate.

And so it went. Call after call. Some better than others. Some were really awkward. (Sorry, Mom.) Many of the calls were to people I had recently met, who had no history with me. I felt guilty about interrupting their routine to ask for business. So I would start with small talk:

"Hey Al, how's Hannah doing?"

"She's great, Ron. Getting excited for the soccer tournament this weekend. What's up?"

"Oh, well, I was just checking in. You know, I recently received my real estate license, and I wanted to know if you knew someone who was buying or selling real estate?"

"No Ron, not now, but I'll keep you in mind."

"Okay. Thanks, Al. Have a great day!"

Alright! Another great call. He said he would keep me in mind.

But it wasn't alright. Al was a friend of mine. His daughter and my daughter played soccer together. I'd see Al at the soccer field and something wasn't quite right. It seemed he would try to avoid me. With each passing month, he didn't answer my calls. As time passed I would find it more and more difficult to make my sales calls.

They actually have a term for it: "call reluctance."

Authors George Dudley and Shannon Goodson, in their book, *The Psychology of Sales Call Reluctance,* describe it this way:

> "Sales call reluctance consists of *all* the thoughts, feelings and avoidance behaviors that conspire to keep otherwise talented, motivated, potential high-level salespeople from ever earning what they're worth."

I'm not sure about the definition, but I know this: I don't like being on the receiving end of a telemarketing call, so how could I, in good conscience, call people to ask for business? I had the guilty feeling of doing something to another person that I don't like being done to me. I think they call it the Golden Rule.

Could there be another way?

THE COACHING INDUSTRY

As I was searching for the answer I came across a training program sponsored by my broker. The class was called "100 Days to Greatness," by sales and coaching guru Brian Buffini. It was supposed to help an agent get their business up and running. Eagerly, I signed up and devoured the content.

Buffini teaches business by referrals. Everyday life presents multiple opportunities to ask for business. At the coffee shop, drop your card to the barista. Don't overlook your waitress at the restaurant, or your drycleaner, or the school principal. All day you have opportunities to connect with people who might know someone who is buying or selling real estate. Always leave your business card, and don't forget to add, "Oh, by the way, I'm never too busy for your referrals" ™. (Seriously, he trademarked that phrase.)

Convinced this was the right way to do business, I signed up for the monthly coaching by Buffini. I would get referral goals to hit each month, monthly newsletters to send to my clients, and—most important—someone to hold me *accountable*.

Accountable for sending out a certain number of handwritten notes. Accountable for making a certain number of calls to people in my sphere of influence. Accountable for having a certain number of lunch appointments. Accountable for sorting my database into A, B, C or D clients. Accountable for doing what they called "pop-bys," which means visiting people in your database with a gift. You pop-by, hand them a gift, and ask for a referral.

This seemed reasonable to me. I actually preferred this to the idea of cold calling or telemarketing. I had a track to run on, a system to implement, something to differentiate myself from other agents.

But I hated it.

The calls were a burden. It just didn't feel right. There were some weeks when I would accomplish my call goals, but not meet my handwritten notes goals. Occasionally, I would make the number of lunch appointments, but rarely would I successfully execute a "pop-by."

You see, I had turned the relationships in my life into prospects. My friends and family had become names and phone numbers on a list. They became my next tasks to accomplish.

Don't get me wrong, I learned a lot from my coach. I learned to redefine success. "Win the day" was a mantra that helped me focus on the task at hand. If you could win three out of five days, you would "win the week." If you could win three out of four weeks you would "win the month." I learned to sort my database by defining the most influential people and focusing my attention on them. I learned that referrals come by earning trust and showing competency. I learned the importance of staying in touch at least monthly.

The Buffini program was an important part of my growth as an agent, but it became a burden each month. I would dread the weekly phone call from my coach. Did you make your calls? Why not? What can we do to help?

With each passing week, the anxiety grew. My business was good, but it wasn't because I was making the necessary calls or sending the requisite number of handwritten notes. The coaching became a negative influence in my life. Every time I would look at my desk and see the checklist of names and numbers, it would cause my blood pressure to rise. I would continually beat myself up for not performing the way I knew that I should. Why would I avoid these calls? What was the source of the *call reluctance?*

I finally realized: I was holding myself accountable for doing things that did not reflect the core of my character. Calling people, even though *I* didn't like to be called, just to make a sale. Superficial relationships through sales calls, notes, lunches, and pop-bys.

There had to be another way.

THE LEAD GENERATION MODEL

I decided to leave the Buffini program for a new way to do business that seemed like a better fit. Instead of making outbound telemarketing calls, I would get interested buyers to call me—attract clients instead of chasing prospects.

Cell phones were catching on and there was a company that offered a call-capture technology using toll-free 800 numbers. The idea was to buy a 1-800 number from them, place it on your real estate signs with "For more info call…" and any caller's phone number would be captured so you could call them back immediately and engage them.

Callers would get a pre-recorded message describing the house for sale and its amenities. They were given the option to connect with an agent. But even if they declined, the listing agent now had their personal cell phone number.

That agent was me. I did not feel right about it at the time. Why? Well, here again, I wouldn't want someone to "capture" my personal cell phone number without my permission. It seemed deceptive. OK, it was deceptive. But, I did it anyway. It's just business.

Sales Mindset. Green Kryptonite.

I promoted this new technology to any home seller who was considering me as their agent. First, I would show them when I walked into the house how the system worked. I would have them call the 1-800 number from their cell phone and watch their face light up when the details of their home were already on the pre-recorded message. Wow! They were impressed. But they were really impressed when I called them right back to ask if they had any questions I could answer about the house. How'd you do that? Magic, smoke and mirrors, deception. But that's just business.

So potential buyers would call my 1-800 number, and I would stop what I was doing and call right away! Imagine the scene: My wife and I are having dinner after a long day at work.

Me: "Sweetheart, this dinner is amazing!"

Ring. Ring. Ring.

My lovely wife Theresa: "Where are you going?"

Me: "Sorry, babe, I'll be right back. Just got a call on the Hurlingham property and I need to call them back."

Ring. Ring. Ring.

Prospect: "Hello?"

Me: "Hi, this is Ron with RE/MAX®. Do you have any questions regarding the house on Hurlingham?"

Prospect: "Uh, no thanks, just checking the price. The recording gave me the details."

Me: "Oh, okay. Let me know if you would be interested in seeing the inside."

Prospect: "Okay, not right now but I'll let you know."

Me: "Great. Are there other properties that you might be interested in? I would be happy to send some to you via email."

Prospect: "No, not right now, thanks."

Me: "Okay, if you need any help with this property or any other, feel free to call me."

Prospect, trying to get rid of me: "Okay, thanks."

Me: "Would it be okay if I followed up a few days?"

Prospect: "Yeah, sure."

Me, hanging up: "Sweet! Wow, another contact. I have their phone number and permission to follow up."

Prospect to his wife: "That was weird. How in the hell did he get my phone number?"

A little deception. *That's* how I got the number. Oh well, it's just business.

But, it's not just business. From the time I first encountered the client I was manipulating them. First, I obtained their cell phone number without permission. They thought they were calling to get information on the property, but didn't know they were giving a sales shark their personal cell number. What if on my signs I added a warning label?

"Caution: If you dial this number you will be giving your personal phone number to a sales shark. This shark will call you, try to get you to give your name and email address for his list of 'prospects.' Once you are on this list, he will call you every few weeks until you buy a house. They will only stop when you have purchased a house."

How many people would dial the number? It seems that deception is a necessary ingredient to this system. But I never slowed down to consider what I was doing. I just needed to make sales and I was susceptible to the *shiny object syndrome.*

Shiny Object Syndrome is an affliction that affects real estate agents. In our haste to grow our business, we buy into the latest and greatest technology for sales. Not just sales, but quick and easy sales. I thought the answer to more clients was technology. Websites, squeeze pages, email campaigns, and of course call capture technology. What I was really doing was looking for the easy sale, the low-hanging fruit.

INTERNET LEADS

As I was contemplating leaving the 1-800 lead generation model, a new and more exciting shiny object emerged.

Zillow is an Internet website where consumers can find houses to purchase and rent. Real estate brokers and homeowners post their homes and consumers can access them on their phone or their home computer. Not only can they find these properties but they can research property values, tax information and more. This traffic for Zillow produces leads.

Zillow makes its money by selling advertising and leads. It allows real estate agents to buy territories for a monthly fee. When a consumer is interested in a particular property, they can, with a click of a button, contact an agent.

This is awesome! You mean, I can pick the area, pay you a monthly fee and get leads to contact *me*? I don't have to call them? They are already interested in real estate? Perfect!

I signed a twelve-month agreement and waited for the leads to come.

At first it was exciting. Prospects would see a house and have questions, but in order to get the information they were after, they had to leave their name, a phone number, and email address. As a Zillow paying advertiser, I would get a text notification with all of that information. A lead to add to my database.

Studies show that the quicker you get back to the customer, the better odds you have to convert them to a client. Many of my peers told me their goal was to call back within five minutes of a notification, so that's exactly what I did. Whatever I was doing at the time became secondary, and my call to the prospect was the new priority. I dialed like I was calling 911 to tell them my house was burning down.

Most of the time they didn't answer. If they did, I tried to set up an appointment to show them the house. Remember: "Real estate is a contact sport," and the best contact is face to face. Showings are a chance to develop the relationship, and hopefully they will get to know me and trust me. Many times, they would be in front of the house and would like to see it *now.*

At first, this lead generation model was so successful that I also signed up with REALTOR.com as well. It had a similar program and the business model was the same, but it had a more streamlined system that provided higher quality leads.

I thought my problem was solved. However, the opposite was true. Yes, they provided leads. Yes, all of the leads were interested in real estate, prequalified in a sense, but none of these leads knew me, liked me, or trusted me. In fact, quite the opposite. I was a stranger, a voice on the phone.

As time passed, my life became miserable. I had succeeded in getting leads. Not just names, phone numbers, and email addresses, but people who were interested in real estate. Everything I did revolved around the next lead. My personal schedule was sacrificed regularly to jump on the next opportunity. I could never relax. I found myself building an incredible list of potential buyers and sellers and my life started to revolve around *them.*

Here's what I learned. These people did not know me, they did not like me, they did not trust me, yet I was rearranging my whole life to chase them. For what? For the possibility of a transaction, a sale? Ah, the sale.

The Sales Mindset. Green Kryptonite.

The number of people who had me show multiple homes and then stopped answering my calls was staggering. I showed a *lot* of homes to folks who had no loyalty to me at all. This caused me to question my own value. I lost self-respect as I tried to prove my worth and value in short three-to-five-minute conversations with total strangers. How in the world can you communicate your value to someone in a three-minute conversation? You can't.

It takes time to learn a person's character and their belief system. Fast talking just doesn't convey the message. Relationships require curation.

You see, it's like dating. Trust doesn't happen day one. You meet a guy at the bar, he comes up to you and asks, "Will you marry me?" That might be a great opening line, and it's sure to get a smile, but who would take it seriously? Over time, with each successive date, trust is built, and after proper curation a relationship develops and a proposal is made.

So it is with client acquisition.

You see, trust is a crucial ingredient to the success of the relationship. Clients who don't value your opinion are not clients at all. Advice is only good if it is followed. I often found myself cajoling my "clients" to do things that I knew were in their best interest, but they would choose another route. This led to experiences that were not good for the client, nor for me as the agent. Most of these people, these leads, did not trust me, but it was not their fault. I don't blame them.

Real estate has a negative reputation. Before most people ever meet a real estate agent they already have a suspicious view of them. Why? Frankly, it's because of the sales mindset taught by most of the brokers in our industry—a mindset that views people as leads, not clients. A mindset that real estate is a numbers game, a contact sport. Telemarketing is seen as normal. Begging for business, normal. Harassing family and friends, normal. Deceiving potential clients, normal. It's just business.

An agent who wants to grow a business gets the same advice from peers, brokers, and the coaching industry: Make more contacts. Hustle. Do more Open Houses. More contacts equal more leads, equals more sales.

There had to be a better way, one that didn't require trading my dignity and self-respect for transactions. One that brought clients to me in a steady and reliable way, without compromising my integrity.

I was miserable with all the chasing. Then, inspired by a sermon at church, I realized my focus was all wrong.

DAREDEVIL EXPERIENCES THE AWAKENING

—ɯ—

First I was blind, but now I see

*"You've got to feel what's **not** there as much as what is."*

-- DAREDEVIL

MATT MURDOCK GREW UP IN Hell's Kitchen, a New York City neighborhood that had a reputation as one of the roughest corners in a tough town.

Raised by his father, "Battlin" Jack Murdock, a tough Irish boxer, Matt learned early in life that sometimes you've got to fight.

His dad wasn't a great boxer and lost more matches than he won. However, he had a reputation for being tough, for taking a beating, and for not quitting. Jack Murdock instilled in his son the importance of doing well in school so he could grow up and avoid fighting for a living. Battlin' Jack wanted a better life for his son.

In order to make ends meet Jack supplemented his boxing earnings by moonlighting for a mobster known as "The Fixer." Jack's work included tanking his regular fights and additional work as an enforcer.

Young Matt Murdock was very close to his father. He idolized him and learned by watching the fights that obstacles in the ring must be overcome with tenacity, determination and grit. But the greatest lesson he learned from his father was how to respond when you get knocked down—to get back up.

One day while walking the streets of New York City, the boy saw an old man who was about to be struck by a moving truck. Matt jumped into the street and pushed the old man out of the way, saving his life. But the truck swerved and crashed, spilling its load of chemicals which splashed on the young boy. His eyes were covered with the toxic chemicals and he was blinded for life.

Encouraged by his father to get up after a "fall," Matt began a long road to recovery. He dedicated himself to learning to read braille and focused on his studies. The accident and the chemicals had some side effects on the young boy. His sense of hearing, touch, taste and smell were super strength. In addition he picked up the ability to "see" via radar.

Battlin' Jack's relationship with "The Fixer" was getting worse. He was being forced to throw his fights instead of trying to win. This didn't sit well with Jack, but because of his desire to provide a better life for his son, he took some falls.

Everything changed with a fight in which Jack was supposed to lose, but he instead disobeyed his mobster boss. Jack wanted his son to witness his dad win a fight, he wanted his respect. No way did he want his son to think that quitting was okay. He wanted to show him that when you get knocked down, you get back up. Quitting is not an option.

Jack won, but his disobedience cost him his life. "The Fixer" took immediate action and killed the elder Murdock.

The loss of his father drove Matt to begin training as a fighter as he also dove into his studies. He wanted to become a lawyer and rid New York of guys like "The Fixer." But eventually his rage drove him to take a different, more direct approach.

Matt's hard work paid off. He was accepted into Columbia University where he earned his law degree. After college he teamed up with his longtime friend Franklin "Foggy" Nelson. Together they opened a law firm.

At the same time, consumed by anger, Matt began planning to avenge his father and bring his killers to justice. He created a costume to hide his identity, and the Daredevil was born. Swiftly the Daredevil brought justice to "The Fixer" and his minions.

Daredevil became a force for good as he continued to fight for justice. Every time he was knocked down, he got back up.

So it is with you, my friend. Before you move forward on your journey to becoming a superhero, you must first work on your fighting skills. Business is a constant battle. You must expect that things won't go well, yet at the same time realize that it's all a part of the process. To be a superhero you must understand that fights will ensue. In order to be prepared for these fights you must develop your skills.

Like you, I knew that the sales culture and getting the easy sale was not a way for me to become a superhero in my community. I needed to focus on building relationships. These relationships would become a superpower with which to change the world.

My skills were weak, so I needed to get started and begin my training regimen. In order to become a superhero, first I needed to work on me.

It all began with a sermon.

My story

The sermon dealt with the Five Capitals. The *American Heritage Dictionary* defines capital this way: "Wealth, especially in the form of financial or physical assets, used in the production or accumulation of more wealth."

So the Five Capitals are the wealth we have in five key areas of life: financial, intellectual, physical, relational, and spiritual. Most of us are familiar with financial capital. You accumulate wealth in the form of money and at some point you can spend it to acquire what you want or need. Well, intellectual capital works the same way. You build intellectual wealth, and deploy it when needed. Same goes for physical, relational, and spiritual wealth.

As I listened to the sermon I realized I had spent most of my time in life chasing the idea of these capitals, but not really focused. I was not intentional about building each of these areas of wealth and consequently did not realize how bankrupt I was in most areas. This was a turning point, an *"aha!"* moment for me. The answer to my dilemma was not out there somewhere. The answer was inside of me. I realized it was time to build into my Five Capitals, to build wealth, to build into myself. My belief was that once I had built up enough reserves in all of these areas the answer would reveal itself.

While listening to the pastor (Chuck Mingo at Crossroads Church in Cincinnati, an absolute rock star communicator), it came to me. A flash of brilliance. An idea that would change the trajectory of my life.

In order to do good in this world, first I needed to be overflowing in these Five Capitals. In essence, I needed to fill my tank, so that I would have the ability to give to others.

- To give great service to my clients, I needed to have physical capital. How can I be sick and on my back in bed and be of any good to anyone?
- In order to give to charities, I needed financial capital. Without money how can I give to my church or to charitable causes?
- To have great relationships, I needed to have relational capital. Without great relationships how can I live a life of meaning?
- To be helpful to others, I needed more intellectual capital. How could I share wisdom if I don't have knowledge?

In order to share God's goodness, I needed spiritual capital. Of course this capital is the most important, for all of wisdom and discernment comes from God. So I began the journey to fill my tank. All five of these capitals are important and valuable. But the one I was most deficient in was intellectual capital.

It was time to *fill up*.

THE FLIGHT SAFETY SPEECH

Wisdom is found in the pre–flight safety speech given by flight attendants all around the globe. The Aviation Reference Guide shows that speech. It goes something like this:

> *"Oxygen and the air pressure are always being monitored. In the event of a decompression, an oxygen mask will automatically appear in front of you. To start the flow of oxygen, pull the mask toward you. Place it firmly over your nose and mouth, secure the elastic band behind your head, and breathe normally. Although the bag does not inflate, oxygen is flowing to the mask. If you are travelling with a child or someone who requires assistance, secure your own mask first, and then assist the other person. Keep your mask on until a uniformed crew member advises you to remove it."*

The pearl of wisdom is here:

> ***".... secure your own mask first, and then assist the other person."***

To make a difference in my business and get off of the treadmill, I needed to work on myself. What good am I to my clients, my family and my neighbors if I have no capital? It was time to put on my *oxygen mask*.

Time to *fill up*.

SEEK AND YOU WILL FIND

The first thing I did was to back out of all of my commitments. I stopped attending meetings and dropped out of my networking group.

If I received an invitation, I declined. My calendar became sacred. My time became off limits to everything that did not fill up my tank.

I became obsessed with finding the track on which to run. I searched the Internet and watched YouTube, looking for inspiration. I listened to podcasts about real estate and other topics. Every night I would fall asleep listening to someone new.

Podcasts are such a good idea. You can go as deep as you want in almost any subject. You can download a program on your iPod or iPhone, put in your earbuds and learn about anything, like listening to a radio program that fits your specific interests and schedule.

Podcasters are mostly experts, such as Tim Ferris who is constantly working toward personal improvement and enlightenment, or James Altucher who is an amazing writer and entrepreneur, Gary Vaynerchuk, who is an expert in social media and business building, and last, but not least, my favorite on real estate and storytelling, Ryan Fletcher.

WHEN THE STUDENT IS READY, THE TEACHER WILL APPEAR
My thirst for intellectual capital accelerated once I started listening to Fletcher. This guy was different. His message was in perfect alignment with me, as I agreed with almost everything he said, especially around messaging. My problem was that I didn't have a message. Hell, I had not even considered a message, how to share it, nor with whom.

Ryan Fletcher runs a company called Agent Marketing Syndicate and his message is like no other. The core is this: To be effective in your business, you must be different, and in order to communicate to others how you are different, you need to become a storyteller.

With these stories you will attract a following of like—minded folks who are attracted to your message. Fletcher, a former copywriter and real estate agent, is an incredible storyteller. In each podcast episode, he delivered high level marketing and business concepts that resonated with me. He encouraged me to stop cold calling, annoying people, or doing things that don't align with the core of my character. Instead, I was encouraged to become a writer, a podcaster, a storyteller. Ryan called agents "beggars." Wow. I had never heard anyone express it in those blunt terms, but I agreed immediately. I had become a beggar.

As I listened to his message on the first few podcasts, I was hooked. I had to hear more. I used almost every free moment to listen to his show. Whether I was doing the laundry, mowing the lawn, washing the dishes, or working out at the gym. With each podcast he would make the case against the real estate industry and the way business is done. The thing that was really compelling to me was his focus on storytelling. Marketing is not just direct mail, websites, squeeze pages, billboards or radio ads. True marketing is good storytelling.

I listened to 56 episodes of the show, falling asleep many nights with earbuds still in my ears. I was so excited to hear about this new way to do business.

Ryan Fletcher saw the real estate business in a different way. He understood the value of relationships, and showed the way to building them with clients. He introduced me to the superpower of relationships as the foundation of a healthy business.

Like the Daredevil, I had to develop the ability to "see" the potential of relationships that I had been blind to for so many years.

In the following chapters, I will attempt to share with you the value of this superpower and how to grow your business focused on relationships while avoiding the pitfalls, pain and frustration of the sales culture. Our journey will take us to a place where we can discover our purpose, not only in business, but in life. Along the way I will share my story and show you how to discover your talents and get them in alignment with a bigger purpose. We will explore the value of stories as your primary marketing tool, and the power of the written word. We will discover ways to tell these stories by building spiritual, physical, relational, intellectual, and financial capital. We will learn the value of walking our own path and how to avoid "shiny object syndrome."

Yes, my friend, you must make a choice: the Sales Mindset or the superpower of relationships?

Let's explore this great truth together.

GREEN ARROW'S PURPOSE DRIVEN BUSINESS

—\\\\\—

Find meaning in your mission

"At my core, I wasn't a *hero*, I was a *hunter*."

-- GREEN ARROW

OLIVER QUEEN WAS A PLAYBOY who inherited millions when his parents died. He spent most of his time seeking the pleasures of life and looking after Number One, never giving much back to society. Over time he accumulated many rivals and enemies until one day while at sea, one of his angry employees pushed him overboard. The world presumed him dead, but he found himself on a deserted island. His survival instinct kicked in and Oliver learned to live off the land by developing hunting skills with his handcrafted bow and arrows.

While on the island he found the remains of a horrible massacre. This shocking experience made him realize that justice was required. He spent the time on the island to hone his skills as a hunter mainly to survive, but as a consequence developed superhuman abilities.

Green Arrow is a superhero. I'm just an ordinary real estate guy. But being a hunter is a great analogy for the sales mindset I used to follow: Always searching for the kill. No empathy for the prey. Pure survival.

You probably don't have superhuman skills with a bow and arrow, either. But maybe we can learn something from Green Arrow.

What did Oliver Queen learn while he was alone on that deserted island? Was he changed by the experience? Did he realize in his solitude that he missed people? That people are important? What about all of those relationships that he took for granted—did he miss them? When his next meal was suddenly his only concern, do you think that gave him a new perspective? Did he maybe realize that the material things in life were not so important? Did he realize that a man needs only a few things to be happy?

Oh, if he could just talk to a human, have a conversation. If only he could have the people back in his life that he so selfishly mistreated. Yet Oliver Queen had more pressing concerns, he had to survive.

Is this where you are in your career? Does the next deal consume you? Like Oliver Queen, are you in survival mode? A hunter?

If this is your story, don't fret, it's not your fault. Many agents, especially newer agents operate in hunting mode. They haven't yet developed their skills, so their methods are awkward and crude. They are taught scripts and cold calling techniques to stalk their prey.

This was my experience as well. I didn't know a better way. Every person to me was merely a name and a number, even my own family members. So each day was a matter of collecting the targeted number of leads. You know, names, numbers, and email addresses, all without purpose.

My purpose in business was to provide for my family—not a bad goal, but also not really a deep purpose. When you are in survival mode, this is a reasonable mindset. However, the approach to your work becomes pointless.

I did my job out of duty. I grudgingly carried my signs to the next open house, followed up with the latest leads, worked the phones. Yeoman like. Stoic.

But sometimes I wondered: What if I did my job, not out of necessity, or out of duty, but from a place of meaning and purpose? How would that look?

Oliver Queen put his creative mind to work and produced his own bow and arrows from the materials he could find on the island. Once he had those basic tools he started to practice, and with committed practice he developed super human skills. What a hunter he became! He could shoot birds on the wing or fish in the sea. And once he mastered his survival skills, he began looking for bigger challenges. He began to look for meaning. And finding meaning led him to becoming someone new. It was the true catalyst that transformed him from playboy Oliver Queen to a superhero, the Green Arrow. He filled his quiver with new weapons, such as glue arrows, grenade arrows, even an atomic warhead arrow. He found his purpose: righting wrongs and fighting for justice.

Maybe you haven't addressed these questions yet in your career: Does your business have a deeper purpose? What outcome do you desire? To make more money? More personal freedom? To influence your community?

Like the Green Arrow, I did not address the question of meaning in my business until I was forced to do so. I was at the end of my rope with the sales culture. I knew there had to be something more than just the next transaction, that there was more to life than just sales and the next deal.

Fortunately, I came across Simon Sinek's book *Start with Why*. Sinek introduced me to the idea that *your Why* should be the starting point for any new business venture. He introduced me to a concept he calls "the Golden Circle."

Essentially, the Golden Circle is a three-ring circle. Think of the Target logo, the retailer's famous bullseye. The outer ring represents *what* a company does, the products or services they provide. The middle ring represents *how* they produce and deliver those products or services. The center circle—the bullseye—represents *why* they do what they do.

In his book, Sinek shows us that most businesses can communicate what they do and how they do it, but can't convey why they do it.

Why do you do what you do?

Don't feel bad if you can't answer this question. Most can't. I couldn't.

Before you can create a business worth doing, or a life worth living, maybe you should consider this question first. Take your time. It's the most important question to answer before moving forward.

Stumbling into my *Why* took much longer than it should have. I really had not given it much thought for the first thirty years of my career. You, my friend, are fortunate. You are discovering this truth now.

How I found my Why

During my self-discovery phase—the "oxygen mask" phase—I went searching for an answer. To my surprise, just the act of seeking, knocking and asking unlocked so many answers for me.

Years ago, I read *The Purpose Driven Life.* In the book, author Rick Warren introduces a question with which most of us struggle. Why am I here? What is my purpose?

The purpose of my business had not yet shown itself, nor had I really considered it. Like most, I had to discover it the hard way, through diligent searching.

During my Five Capitals training described in Episode 3, I realized that every agent, every person, needs to be healthy in their spirit, intellect, and body in order to operate to their fullest.

So one day I was having coffee with one of my agents when I found myself saying something that would change my life forever.

I was recapping a conversation I had with my mother only a few days earlier. Mom and I were discussing forgiveness. Specifically, she thought I was angry with a family member and was holding a grudge. This particular family member had a very negative impact on me and I decided staying away was maybe the best decision.

"Mom, I don't have a grudge, in fact, I have a superpower—I truly want every person I meet to be successful in life. If (this family member) showed up tomorrow and wanted to continue our relationship, I would do everything I could to encourage them."

As I was having coffee with my agent, I blurted out the same line: "I have a superpower—I truly want everyone I meet to be successful in life."

I realized that my superpower was empathy. Said another way, it's a ***coach's mindset***. One who truly is emotionally committed to the success of the player and the team.

My mission was coming into view. Whatever my *Why* would be, it would include coaching.

Meanwhile, the questions kept coming: Why am I doing this? Why do I want to continue growing my business? What's the bigger purpose?

As I reflected and searched my soul for the answers, I realized that I had a passion for helping kids. I started to think maybe I could use my business to impact the lives of kids in my community. This was a much bigger purpose-driven approach.

But how? Where? For whom?

HIT THE HEART OF THE TARGET

The answer, when it came, was like Green Arrow's trick boomerang arrow. It came from my past and hit the bullseye in my heart.

You see, my childhood was one of chaos. Growing up in poverty without a father for most of my childhood impacted me in many ways. Above all, people need security. Especially kids. They need certainty.

But certainty was far from my daily reality. Because of my mother's circumstances I attended four different schools by the time I finished the third grade. Moving regularly impacted me in so many ways, most of them quite negatively. Being the new kid, trying to fit in, constantly trying to prove myself, put me in the mindset of an outsider. A misfit. Not good enough.

My life was inconsistent in so many ways. Everything to me seemed temporary. Relationships, my current house, my next surrogate father— in my heart I knew nothing good would last.

Over time the conditions in the apartments where we lived got worse. As in many government subsidized projects, the residents had no reason to care for their apartments. They had no financial stake in the success of the project, so decline was inevitable. Our complex became known for drugs, violence, and total chaos.

Meanwhile, the quality of the people who moved in seemed to decline as well. I was exposed to very adult themes at a tender age. In many ways I feel like I had the innocence of childhood taken from me. For years I suffered from nightmares. I felt unprotected. Insecure.

Reflecting on my dark and unhappy past made me realize the mission I was most passionate about: Protecting children. Like the comic-book heroes I followed to escape my pain and fear, I want to do something about injustice and protect the innocent.

That is my purpose.

I believe that children need to know that their parents will protect them. That no matter the circumstances, they will always be there. There to provide, there to protect, there to comfort.

That was not true for me. As a child, I never felt like I was safe. I never felt protected. That made me emotionally unstable, ungrounded. I was angry, but I didn't know why.

What does this have to do with business?

What if my business could help me reach out to people in my community with the sole purpose of finding the kids who are facing what I faced as a child? Kids who are in the midst of chaos, kids who need a protector?

Revisiting Simon Sinek's "Golden Circle," I finally put it all together.

The following message is on my whiteboard in my office to this day:

What: Real Estate

How: Relationships Through Storytelling

Why: Impact Kids in my Community

My Big *Why* was now in focus.

Like Oliver Queen, I had to experience some harsh things to truly understand how to survive and find meaning for my life, meaning for my business.

Maybe this is true for you as well. Do you have a sense of your *Why*?

Nothing yet? That's okay.

Episode 11 of this book deals with taking action regarding your Big *Why*. There are some very concrete steps you can take to uncover your purpose, but for now, let's allow your subconscious mind to work on this issue while we move on to a subject that might help you clarify.

Let's move on to Self-Awareness.

CAPTAIN AMERICA SHOWS SELF-AWARENESS

—ɯ—

Find your secret identity

"Doesn't matter what the press says. Doesn't matter what the politicians or the mobs say. Doesn't matter if the whole country decides something wrong is something right. This nation was founded on one principle above all else: the requirement that we stand up for what we believe, no matter the odds or consequences. When the mob and the press and the whole world tell you to move, your job is to plant yourself like a tree beside the river of truth, and tell the whole world—'No, YOU move.'"

-- CAPTAIN AMERICA

STEVE ROGERS WAS BORN JULY 4th, 1922 in lower East Manhattan. A survivor of polio, he was a frail and very small young man.

As the United States entered World War II, the young Rogers was inspired to join the army to fight the Nazis but was too small and too weak to be accepted. Undaunted, the young man applied over and over again.

He caught the attention of General Chester Phillips who offered entry to a top-secret experiment called Operation Rebirth. The goal of the program was to create an army of physically superior soldiers. As the first human test subject, Rogers was given a "Super Soldier Serum" and then was exposed to "Vita-Rays" that activated the chemicals in his system.

Captain America was born.

He was one of the original comic-book superheroes who fought the Germans and Japanese during World War II, then came home to make the world a better place.

What makes a scrawny, sickly young man think that he can fight? What kind of push-back would he have gotten from his friends and family?

Steve Rogers was a little guy, with a disabled body, but his strength came from the inside. His inner voice was strong and pushed him forward. He showed that action combined with faith is a powerful force, and that simple persistence finally put him in a position to get noticed by the right person. General Phillips no doubt chose Rogers for Operation Rebirth not only because of his enthusiasm to serve, but because he showed up again and again. Rejection was not final for this young man as he brushed off disappointment and kept his eyes on the goal—serving his country and defeating the Nazis.

Rogers was a fighter. Even if no one else believed it, he knew it himself. He had self-awareness.

Knowing yourself—your talents and your strengths—is at the heart of self-awareness. But it's not easy. Honestly evaluating that person in the mirror is difficult for most of us.

What is your identity? Or, better said, what do you *believe* about your identity? What about your natural point of aim? Where are you strong? What are your weaknesses?

MY JOURNEY TO AWARENESS

Before launching my business full scale I needed to answer these questions. Once I determined the changes I hoped to make in the world by discovering my purpose, I turned my attention toward self-awareness.

As a football coach, I learned that you should take players and put them in positions that will allow them to succeed. If you have a kid who is three hundred pounds, you probably won't use him at running back or defensive back. Those positions require speed and agility, not the strong suit for a heavyweight. But he might be an excellent lineman. Why? Because it's his natural point of aim, his strength.

Determined to better understand my strengths, I made a really important decision: Whatever I discovered about myself, I would accept it, and I would work on that set of skills and talents until I was exceptional. In other words, I decided to go "all in" on my strengths and not give my weaknesses the time of day. Instead, I would find people who could do the things that don't fit my strengths and skills.

Self-awareness starts with honesty. You have to be honest with yourself, and get honest opinions from those around you who are courageous enough to tell you the truth, because an outside view can be more objective.

Falling asleep every night with my earbuds still in was a nightly occurrence, part of my mission to find meaning in my business and meaning in my life. Of course, I was listening to podcasts. One Thanksgiving I woke up at 5:00 a.m., suddenly wide awake. I was inspired to write down everything in my life that described who I was, and all that I aspired to achieve. My passions.

In order to identify passions, I realized I had to only include things that brought real emotion. No grays, no pastels, but only bold colors and black and white. I knew the time for half–steps had passed. It was time to get real.

What did I love? What did I hate? These questions required me to go deep.

Love and hate are clarifying words. We truly don't *love* very many things, nor do we truly *hate* that many. When making a list of them, you are forced to be honest and truly say that you love something or identify what you hate. Making a list of things you don't like and those that you "kinda like" does not have the same level of passion. This exercise made me realize that living in the passions, love or hate, is the essence of motivation.

So I wrote it all down. I carefully studied the descriptive words that truly elucidated things in life for which I was passionate.

In the end there were four pages of notes and ideas. The words on those pages elicited strong emotional reactions. I described myself as a warrior, creative, courageous, angry, passionate. I wrote: "I love to coach; to do things the right way; I want *everyone* to succeed; I want people to be healthy and prosperous, positive, fulfilled."

The coach inside of me was stepping out. I wrote down other descriptive phrases:

"I love my country, I love life, I love Jesus, baseball, basketball, martial arts, good design, color, good music, football, people, kids especially, elderly especially... " The list went on: "competitive, overcomer, good communicator, I am a good writer, speaker..."

On my hate list was a word that jumped off the page. A word that evoked a visceral reaction: *injustice.*

Yes, I hate injustice. One person treating another person unfairly. Taking advantage. Abusive. A person or group controlling others for personal gain. Keeping individuals from pursuing their dreams.

This was the one word that elicited the strongest emotion. Recognizing my reaction to injustice was the beginning of awareness about what made me tick. Understanding what motivated me was an important step on my path to self-awareness.

As I studied all of the words, my talents and passions were coming into focus. I was starting to get the picture.

As I reviewed my notebook, I felt like my future was unveiling itself. I was not sure how all of those disparate ideas would come together, yet I was encouraged. Finally, I had honestly put on paper my passions and skills. Now, if only I could figure out how to incorporate them into my life.

How did things as unlike and far apart as Jesus, martial arts, and writing make any sense? What did they have to do with how I would grow my business and make a difference on this planet? Nowhere on my list were the words "real estate," "selling," "conversion rates," "return on investment," "key performance indicators," or "lead generation."

Interesting.

FIND YOUR NORTH STAR

Looking back at that list was the first time in my forty-eight years where I could actually start to get an idea of who I was as a person—the things that got me excited, my passions, my pain.

And like therapy, my list highlighted the adults in my life who hurt me or abandoned me. It was hard to revisit that pain when I made my lists, but that is how honest you should be when writing your passions. Don't leave anything out. All of it matters.

Next I wondered: How could I use the pain of my youth for good in the world? What the heck did it have to do with my business? At that point it wasn't clear, but somehow I knew it would become clear as I began to design my life. Not just my personal life, but also my business life.

Just like scrawny Steve Rogers who kept showing up no matter how many times he was rejected, when everyone told him his dream would never come true, I had to push on and have faith that it would work out, that determination and persistence would win in the end.

Which brings me to a very important part of self-awareness and mapping your future: one life.

ONE LIFE

My life was full of pretense. I had multiple personalities. Not in a clinical sense, but like most people: While working I behaved a certain way, yet a different way at home, and yet a different way at church. I was the pretender, always trying to fit in. I felt like an outsider. I cared too much what people thought about me. I was insecure.

I was taught that personal life and business life should be kept separate, that you shouldn't mix work and pleasure or do business with family, and that church and state should be kept separate. But none of it was true. I discovered that there was no "business life" or "personal life." There was only one life. And it was mine to design. My boss, my parents, my wife, my family—they didn't get to define me. The definition of my life was mine for the making.

Self-discovery brought me to the realization that my talents, skills, and mindset should be deployed together in concert. Only this time, I was the conductor. Not my clients, not my wife, not my family, not the groups to which I belonged, not my church, not my peers. No, this time, the real me, the person looking back from my notebook, on these four pages, this person, *he* was going to take the lead.

No longer was my spiritual life a secret from my clients. No longer was I a different person on Sunday than the one you met on Monday. No longer did I try to fit into the group, or behave for others. It was time to live according to the passions God gave me by design and experience— the talents and life-shaping experiences unique to me.

It all became crystal clear.

I knew where I wanted to go. I would not follow someone else or pay a guru to tell me what to do next. I would look in the mirror and uncover the real me.

Reflection and a self-audit helped me discover that I was a purebred entrepreneur, a fighter, a protector, and a coach.

Self-awareness brought me to the truth—that I was designed to create and I was here to fight. My company, my business was mine to create. My passion was to fight against injustice. My business became the creative outlet that allowed me to make a positive impact on the world around me.

What are you here to do? What do your skills and passions tell you about what you should be doing? Should you start a business? Should you join someone else's? Should you create art? Should you build things with your hands? Maybe you are better suited to be a manager, not creating, but making sure of compliance. Maybe you should be teaching and not in business, or maybe you can teach within your business.

No one saw Steve Rogers as a warrior, but *he* knew who he was even though it was not obvious to the rest of the world. Is there a Captain America inside of you that nobody else sees? Is there a burning desire that consumes you? Do you have a superhero inside that wants to make the world a better place?

There is no such thing as Super Soldier Serum. The amazing Vita-Ray chamber exists only in the pulp pages of old comic books. But you have access to a device that is just as powerful: self-discovery. Do the audit, my friend. Discover your natural point of aim and combine it with your big *Why*. With passions, purpose and skills all aligned, you will be ready to make a difference.

Start by making your own list: love and hate. At first, it might feel a little weird. But believe me, that's a small price to pay for finding your "North Star," your natural point of aim. What we're trying to do here is reset and recalibrate so you can move forward with clarity and conviction toward a life worth living.

Think it over, sleep on it. Let your subconscious mind work on this issue over time. Becoming self-aware comes more naturally to some, but we all have the ability to become more objective if we will just let the pen and paper show us the way.

Just being interested will not get you closer to your passion. As Captain America said, you have to take your stand by the river of truth. Don't hide behind your shield. Use it like he does, to win your battles. Put down on paper those things that bring emotional responses, to discover your passions in life.

Self-discovery doesn't just happen by flipping a switch. Don't expect to have a spontaneous clarifying light-bulb moment that answers all of your questions about your talents and goals and passions. Discovering who you are is best accomplished by actually *doing* something.

Once you have determined your Big *Why* and understand your strengths and weaknesses through self-discovery, it will be time to take the next step.

Every superhero has a story. In the next chapter, we will build yours.

CAPTAIN MARVEL AND THE POWER OF WORDS

—ιιι—

Find your secret identity

*"Give me a Superman, only have his other identity be
a 10- or 12-year-old boy rather than a man."*

-- ROSCOE KENT FAWCETT, CREATOR OF CAPTAIN MARVEL

FOSTER KIDS DON'T HAVE IT easy.

That was the case for Billy Batson. Orphaned at a young age he was not like most foster kids. His primary goal in life was not to find a family, but to turn eighteen, get out on his own, and become an adult. He was tired of being helpless and unwanted, at the mercy of adults who could shuffle him from home to home.

Although he was a compassionate and kind boy, to protect himself he learned to stay emotionally distant from everyone. He formed no attachments because they usually led to a broken heart.

But Billy's life changed dramatically when he met a wizard who introduced him to a powerful word: "Shazam!"

That magical word contained:

"S" for the wisdom of Solomon.

"H" for the strength of Hercules.

"A" for the stamina of Atlas.

"Z" for the power of Zeus.

"A" for the courage of Achilles.

"M" for the speed of Mercury.

And by speaking that word, Billy Batson, the lonely, vulnerable, insecure foster child, was transformed into the powerful adult superhero known as Captain Marvel.

During the 1940s, when comics were king among kids, Captain Marvel was more popular than Superman and slugged it out with the "Man of Steel" in epic battles before he was finally defeated by lawyers in copyright infringement cases.

But his magic word, which also became interchangeable as his name, remains: "Shazam!" And that's a lesson that everyone in business or any walk of life should embrace:

Words have superpowers. They are among the most powerful forces on Earth.

Simple words such as "Yes" and "No" change careers and lives. They can make a dream come true or break a heart.

We pledge our love and commitment in matrimony with two words: "I do."

Wars are launched and lives are lost with a single word: "Fire!"

God's grace, healing and forgiveness can begin with two words: "I believe."

So if you believe in the power of words, why not learn more about it? Why not harness it to accomplish your goals? You can use words to grow your business, to make your life better, to make the world a better place.

Billy Batson tapped into the power of a single word, but as business leaders and marketers our power lies in the ability to put together words in a way that wields the most influence—by telling a story.

Stories are the way that people have communicated throughout human history. The greatest storytellers have created movements that have rocked the world and transformed the future. Jesus, the Founding Fathers, Shakespeare, Homer, Winston Churchill, all were incredible storytellers.

Words that were inspired by ideas were stitched together in a message, and then told through stories that changed the course of history.

All of the major religions began with stories. Jesus changed history with His story that God valued relationships with people so highly that He gave His Son that they might believe and be saved. The world has never been the same. Even our daily calendar reflects His life and death.

Christianity has touched billions of people and is still changing lives today. As it says in the Book of John: "In the beginning was the Word…" (John 1:1)

George Washington, Thomas Jefferson, Ben Franklin, John Adams—these men who bravely stood up to the ruling monarchy, knowing full well that their lives were on the line—all believed in a message. It was written, documented, inked on paper and signed by them: The Declaration of Independence. These words, and the ideas that they represented created a new nation that became the greatest in the history of man. Jefferson and his commission of five who wrote the Declaration of Independence forever changed the world. Their truths are still self-evident.

Churchill was one of the great thinkers, writers, and communicators in history. During the dark days of World War II, it was his voice that gave hope to the British people as the Nazis rained bombs, fire and rockets on Great Britain. As Prime Minister he understood that the free people of the world, starting with his own nation, faced an existential threat—Hitler was coming.

Churchill turned to God and one of the most effective weapons of war, the carefully written word.

"I have nothing to offer but blood, toil, tears and sweat…" Churchill said.

"We have before us an ordeal of the most grievous kind. We have before us many, many long months of struggle and of suffering. You ask, what is our policy? I can say: It is to wage war, by sea, land and air, with all our might and with all the strength that God can give us; to wage war against a monstrous tyranny, never surpassed in the dark, lamentable catalogue of human crime. That is our policy. You ask, what is our aim? I can answer in one word: It is victory, victory at all costs, victory in spite of all terror, victory, however long and hard the road may be; for without victory, there is no survival."

That speech and others gave hope to a battered nation in its darkest days, and rallied the rest of the allies to battle and defeat Hitler's death machine. Churchill's words were not just random. He carefully crafted them and delivered them to those who needed to believe they could win. His leadership, revealed by his words, saw Great Britain through its longest night.

OK, so you and I are not Winston Churchill or William Shakespeare. We're just trying to sell houses, or cars, or dry-cleaning services or communicate better at work and at home. So where do stories fit into our business?

Just like Billy Batson saying "Shazam!" we have access to an incredible superpower. But like everything else in life, it's not enough to just think about it. We need to speak up, to make a decision to act. Commit to learn the craft. Commit to understanding its power. Commit to harnessing it. Commit to becoming a great storyteller.

My origin story

It was the spring of 1975. My mom had just separated from her second husband. We landed in the quaint river town of Loveland, Ohio in government subsidized apartments. My three younger brothers and my older sister and I were fascinated with our new apartment. It was warm. Everything was new. We had a bedroom for the boys, a bedroom for my sister, and one for my mom. We even had indoor plumbing.

We had just moved from my grandmother's house in Montgomery, Ohio where we needed to stay until my mom could get things sorted out. Grandma's house was very small, lightly insulated, with no indoor plumbing. There was a pump in the basement to draw water from a well for cooking, drinking, and cleaning. The outhouse was behind the house and down a trail. To a 7-year-old boy, that trip was scary, especially at night, especially in the cold. I had to take a flashlight to find my way.

That journey to the outhouse wasn't far, but I traveled it alone. At night. And now I now realize, that's how I became independent and self-reliant at 8 years old.

In time, my stepdad reconciled with my mother and moved into our new apartment.

I soon discovered that he read and collected comic books that were stacked up in the closet four feet high. They were an escape for a young boy. This was my introduction to superheroes. Protecting people, saving the innocent, punishing the evildoers. I was hooked!

I would grab one and read it for hours at a time in the corner of my bedroom. I was fascinated with the art, the fantasy and the stories. The experience was thrilling, exciting and engrossing.

First I would carefully study the front cover, reading every word. Then I would turn it over and study the back cover. Satisfied, I would open it up and enter a new world. I would read every page and study every drawing until the story was exhausted, then I would read the advertisements in the back. Charles Atlas offered the body-building secrets of "dynamic tension" in ads like, "The Insult that

Made a Man out of Mac," showing a 98-pound weakling who becomes a musclebound hero after getting sand kicked in his face at the beach. Or you could order exciting "Sea Monkeys," which appeared to be some sort of exotic aquatic creature you could keep as a pet, but were actually just unhatched brine shrimp. (Did you know that May 16 is National Sea Monkey Day?)

But the ads that excited me were the ones that shouted, "Run Your Own Business!" I picked one from a seed company, filled out the coupon, mailed it in, and I was in business.

I didn't know the first thing about selling. (At 8 years old, what *do* you know about anything?) I would take my seeds and go door–to–door in my apartment complex and try to sell them. This type of selling required hustle, but it seemed simple to me: Offer your seeds, give them the price, ask for the sale. It worked! Making sales was easy!

It's funny looking back after so many years: Why in the world would someone want seeds in an apartment complex? Hardly anyone had a garden. But I just kept knocking on doors, offering products that no one wanted!

SALES CULTURE CIRCA *1975*

As adults, we sometimes lose track of our humanity. We have a job to do. Potential customers are nothing more than obstacles on the path to success. This is the essence of the Sales Mindset. Doing whatever it takes to get the next sale. I caught on quickly. I annoyed people by knocking on their doors, unannounced, to sell them something they weren't interested in. I didn't want a relationship with them, I just wanted their money. I just wanted a sale.

One can forgive an 8-year-old for that. But real estate agents are doing this today. Not only are they knocking on doors, they are cold calling, telemarketing, using bait–and–switch tactics—all condoned by their brokers and trainers. All to get a sale. A transaction. So focused on getting the sale, they abandon everything they learned in kindergarten and treat people like objects.

Door knocking, as it turns out, is not the answer. Nor is telemarketing, or email spam.

So, what is the answer?

Words.

Although I was inspired by the advertisements in the comics to pursue business, it wasn't until many years later that I was introduced to the idea that I, like Billy Batson, could put the power of words to use in business and tell my own stories.

FLETCH INTRODUCES ME TO STORYTELLING
I have come to believe that words are the most powerful force on Earth.

Throughout my career I had ignored this great power. Honestly, I wasn't really aware of it. I gave little thought to writing or communicating to my clients. My idea of a message was a text, an email, or a handwritten note.

You see, what I realize now is that we (as human beings) are always communicating with our clients or future clients. The way we dress, our posture, the words we choose when speaking. It's all storytelling.

Within the sales culture no one practices or teaches the value of story-telling. Although it is the most important subject when trying to earn business, it gets almost no attention. This is not only true in real estate but also in many other industries.

Were it not for Ryan Fletcher, I would still not be a student and practitioner of storytelling. Ryan, whom I mentioned in Episode 3, is one of the best storytellers and communicators I have ever encountered. His background was that of a copywriter, and he has a unique ability to put messages inside of a story that really moved me.

"Fletch," as I like to call him, is special. But, what do I know?

Growing up in the late seventies and early eighties, I carefully observed the great communicators. It's one of the topics that fascinates me. As a sports fan I paid particular attention to the great announcers—Howard Cosell as he did the great boxing matches and Monday Night Football. Bob Costas, Bryant Gumbel, Keith Jackson, and of course the voice of the Cincinnati Reds, the great Marty Brennaman.

After starting a family I became interested in politics—after all, I had to make sure the world was a better place for my children. I became a careful observer of the great communicators such as Presidents Ronald Reagan and Bill Clinton or Newt Gingrich, Speaker of the House in the mid-1990s. I would watch the Sunday political shows just to hear the words and messages spoken by these political leaders with the sole intent to expand my vocabulary.

All of these men were amazing communicators. And Ryan Fletcher has world class communication skills, just like these men. What do I know? I only know talent when I see it.

Once I started the journey toward changing my life, and "putting on the oxygen mask", I stumbled across Ryan's YouTube channel where he was decrying the evils of the real estate industry and its cadre of door knockers, telemarketers, and slick salespeople.

The YouTube channel also promoted his website. Intrigued, I switched over to his site where I saw a four-part video series that opened my eyes to the great truth of the power of words. In this video series, Fletcher introduced me not only to the power of words but also to the idea that real estate agents should focus on the most powerful idea in the business—the idea of being a protector.

"A protector!" I thought. "That's what I've been saying! For years! Hell, I named my company Bastion for that very reason! Okay Fletch, now you have my attention, what else do you believe?"

Sure enough, this guy had more than marketing gimmicks and platitudes. This dude was deep. He had done his homework. Somewhere in his marketing he mentioned his podcast, and I started listening.

Wow.

As talented a writer as he was, I think his delivery as an orator was almost as impressive. The subject matter of the show wrapped around the idea that storytelling should be at the core of your business marketing. Storytelling to make connections. Crafting messages that resonate with your readers (prospects, as we called them in the sales culture). For what reason? To build relationships.

Messages? Writing? Attracting an audience? Relationship building? Why had I not considered this? What had I been doing all of these years?

I had been prospecting. Looking for the next transaction. Stuck in the sales mindset.

As I listened to each show my mind started racing. I felt like I had found the Holy Grail—storytelling to build relationships—and I knew this was the path for me.

Fletcher's relentless assault on the sales culture and its coaches and his remedy of storytelling for relationships had me excited. But how could it be done? How could I learn to tell stories? I was no writer!

PATH TO WRITING

Storytelling in business starts with beliefs. In my entire career I had never written down what I believed. Before I could begin to tell a story to my audience I had to think about what it was that I believed. What principles did I hold?

These beliefs make up the core of your message.

You are probably asking yourself, "My message? What is my message? I have to have a message before I begin to market? You mean I don't just pick up a phone and call people? You mean I can't just have an open house and meet my next client? I need a message?"

I had the same questions. I didn't have a message, because I had not considered it. Agents can go through their entire career and not have a message. All they need is the next transaction. I had lived that life for thirteen years, and it had led me to a very dark place. The time had come for change.

So I started to study writing, crafting messages, and communication.

The beauty of our current technology (primarily the Internet and the smartphone) is that books, podcasts, and blogs are easy to find. With a Google search you can find information on almost any subject with a few clicks of the mouse.

I started to pay attention to great stories. I found them in movies, books, and from marketers who were deploying this skill already. People like Fletch.

Writing down my beliefs on a piece of paper was magical. It became more clear to me how I would craft my message. But beliefs alone were not enough. My personal story had to be woven into my overall message, and that message has to be authentic. My story had to be told.

My personal experiences, talents, skills, were all important parts of my story. So I thought about my history, my pains, my successes. These helped me better understand myself. As I mentioned with the self-awareness experience in Episode 5, these writings were like looking into a mirror. My story was writing itself.

You see, your personal history and experiences are unique to you. They make your fingerprint in the universe. Combined with your beliefs, these memories and experiences make up the scaffolding of your message.

Mine reminded me that I came from a life of chaos. A childhood that was out of control. Looking at my experiences on a sheet of paper re-minded me that I had experienced a lot of rejection, that I was unpro-tected as a child, that I deeply longed for a hero, someone who would have my back.

It became clear to me why Fletcher's message of a protector was so attractive to me. I had behaved as a protector my entire adult life, first to my wife, then to my kids, driven in part by my experiences as a child.

My story (the life of chaos) combined with my beliefs (personal freedom and the duty to protect) helped build my message. It was not just a message for my business, but a message for my life.

The power of a word changed everything for Billy Batson. By saying "Shazam!" he was transformed into a superhero who could conquer anything, even Superman. The right words are waiting for you, too. If you have looked into the mirror of self-awareness and identified your mission and purpose, you are ready to tell your story. And that will be the core of building your message and ultimately in building relationships, which is the key to success in business and in life. Your story brings them all together in one life.

The creators of Captain Marvel chose to make their "Clark Kent" a 10-year-old boy because they knew that would appeal most to the readers of comic books. The story of Captain Marvel was a story about all 10-year-old boys who sit under a shade tree reading comics while they long to grow up and be more powerful. And that is true for your story, too. Parts of your story will be true for others. They will recognize some of their own life experiences in your story. They will see that you both have something in common, and that is the start of building a relationship.

Later, we will discuss how to write and craft your story. But first, let's talk about how to communicate. The best story ever written is pointless if nobody ever reads it. So how do you get the word out?

That's our next step: "Shazam!"—the creation of media.

BATMAN DEPLOYS MEDIA

—ɯ—

A tool for your Bat-Belt

"Everything's impossible until somebody does it.'

-- BATMAN

BRUCE WAYNE WAS BORN TO Dr. Thomas Wayne and his wife, Martha, wealthy socialites in Gotham City. Privileged as a child, he grew up in Wayne Manor with his every need met.

That all changed when at the age of 8 he lost his parents. On a dark night, walking home from the movie theater, they were confronted by a petty criminal, who shot and killed them.

The young boy vowed to rid the world of criminals and began training. Fighting crime would require exceptional physical abilities so he started fitness training and martial arts studies. Simultaneously, through intense scientific study and research, he developed an incredible mind.

Developing these skills made him a formidable opponent.

Early on he decided to do his crime fighting on his own, as the police might not mete out justice to his liking. In essence, he decided to become a vigilante. This would require a mask and a secret identity.

While contemplating his secret identity he saw a bat fly into the room. "That's it!" he thought. "Dark, creature of the night—I'll strike terror into the hearts of these criminals. I'll dress like a bat!"

Batman was born.

Unlike Superman and Spider-Man, he had no supernatural powers. Driven by the traumatic memory of his parents' murder and driven with vengeance on his mind, he vigorously developed his skills. His motivation, his Big *Why*, was clear. To supplement his already sharp mind and physical abilities, he created an incredible array of tools with which to fight the villains. His famous utility belt carried items such as grappling hooks, lock picks, or his gas mask.

Weapons in his arsenal also included the Batmobile, his helicopter called the Batcopter, and of course his secret lair, the Batcave, connected to Wayne Manor by a secret tunnel and used as his Batman headquarters, where he kept his crime lab and all of his latest Bat-gadgets.

These tools, combined with natural talents and highly developed skills, transformed Bruce Wayne into Batman, a superhero. So it can be with you.

Batman started by creating his own story. Your business needs your story—your Big *Why*, your differentiation point. Once your story is developed, it has to be told.

But how?

As an individual, you are limited. You only have so much time, and you can only reach so many people. But like Batman, you can leverage the communication skills you already possess and access the powers of a superhero. First by telling your story; then by using the greatest tool in the storyteller's utility belt: *media.*

Media was once defined by radio, television, newspapers, magazines or billboards. This is still partly true and all of these vehicles are still valid. However, in today's wired and connected world, the media we will focus on is media that can be shared readily via the Internet.

Let's start with media in written form, such as websites, blogs, news-letters, and books. Then there is media in digital audio form, such as mp3's or even CD's. And finally, media in the form of pictures or video.

Without media, your story, your cause, is limited in its reach. What good is a great story if no one hears it? How can they join the fight if they don't hear or understand the story?

In Episode 6 we discussed the importance of story and how a story al-lows you to share your beliefs with your audience, your potential cus-tomers and clients.

Media allows you to leverage those ideas and beliefs, in order to scale your business. With media you can record your message once and share it with the world multiple times.

MY STORY

When I was with Payless Cashways, we had access to all of the media outlets at the time. The corporation had strategies in place for newspapers, radio, television and billboards. Each week they would promote the business and bring people in by leveraging these great tools. Although expensive, this type of advertising was the only way to reach customers at great scale: One-to-many communication.

Another way to reach customers was to hire salespeople. One-to-one communication.

As a sales manager, that was my job.

As you might expect at a lumberyard, many of the customers were building contractors. These customers would purchase some of their daily materials but also spent a lot of money at supply houses that were more focused on their specific discipline. For example, many of the home builders would buy their lumber and framing materials at the local family-owned lumberyards.

Our company addressed this challenge by hiring sales reps who would be charged with networking with these builders in order to develop relationships and grow the business.

In those days we did not have social media, so almost all of my training was predicated on the tools of the day: the telephone, pen and paper, and the car.

I was taught, and then taught my salespeople, that their job each day was simple: schedule as many face-to-face meetings with prospects and customers as possible.

Every day would require a telephone, a list, and a whole lot of tenacity. We used cold calls, warm calls and handwritten notes. These were the habits of a good salesman. Most salespeople, it turns out, even the best salespeople, hated making the calls. It was a chore, drudgery. It wasn't until I got into the real estate business that I learned why this activity is so hated. By the way, not just hated by the person making the calls, but also by those on the receiving end!

My business practices in real estate were much the same as the practices taught to my sales reps at the lumberyard.

You see, media was not a consideration for a beginning real estate practitioner. Newspaper ads, television ads and radio were all very expensive. Not to mention they were not very targeted. So I turned to the least expensive and most direct path to getting sales: the telephone.

THE TELEPHONE AS A SALES TOOL
The telephone as a medium is a paradox. The phone call is tantalizing, as it seems like it is the shortest distance between two points. Speed.

The goal as I began each day was to make a certain number of sales calls. From these calls I would have only one goal: to schedule a face-to-face appointment.

The list of potential clients came from FSBO's (For-Sale-By-Owner), expired listings, past clients, and my "sphere of influence" (friends and family).

Communicating with people via the telephone is one-to-one and is fraught with problems. The biggest problem is in the area of building a relationship.

In essence, that's what salespeople are doing with a phone call: trying to shortcut the relationship cycle. No relationship, no romance, no sale.

First, calling anyone is an interruption. People don't want to be interrupted. I would call and my intent was clear, to get appointments. The call was all about me, selfish. There wasn't a clear benefit to the person who received the call.

The person on the other end of the phone did not need me, otherwise they would be calling me, not the other way around. So my job, in a short conversation, was to convince the person on the other end of the phone that they: a) had a problem; and b) I was the solution. With no context and no history with the person, I had an uphill battle. Most of the time I was calling someone who had no history with me, didn't know me, like me, or trust me.

This is the great lie of the sales culture, that it is actually possible to get someone to know, like, and trust you in three- to five-minute conversations. This lie has led a lot of sales professionals to a life of frustration, depression, and desperation.

Nevertheless, I persisted. I was taught to make the contacts. "Remember, real estate is a *contact sport*," they would say. "It's a numbers game."

Telemarketing.

That's not what my sales coaches called it, but that's what it is. Every time I picked up the phone to call someone to get business, in essence I had become a telemarketer.

FACE-TO-FACE APPOINTMENTS

It was very difficult to get meetings with anyone. Once I did land an appointment, it always went the same way. I would spend the entire time trying to convince the prospect that I was competent, that I was trustworthy, and that my services were a good value.

Having never considered developing my story, much less putting it in writing, I would just lean on my years in sales, focusing on active listening skills and obfuscation. Most of these meetings ended in failure as it was nearly impossible to convey my story, even with thirty to sixty minutes. The prospect could not truly understand my value proposition, and they did not have any context for me or for my business. And I'm not sure I understood my value proposition, either.

What if there was a way to get this kind of context across to the general public? What if I could tell stories that demonstrated my character? How could I get them out to customers?

THE POWER OF MEDIA

To give context to your prospects, you need content: Content that tells your story and gives them the full context of who you are as a person and as a business.

This is the power of media coupled with story.

Instead of calling your prospects, you can invite them to watch your video that explains your value proposition. Or you can send them to your website or your blog that lays out your business philosophy and the story of how your business came to be. Instead of meeting one-to-one, you can mail them a copy of your book that conveys your business religion in story form. Maybe you write and mail a monthly newsletter that over time conveys your story and reveals your character.

You see, media can do the heavy lifting of bringing full context to any meeting you might have. With media you can build relationships over time by sharing stories.

Just a short time ago, media was inaccessible to the average person. We are so fortunate to live in a time where it's never been easier to access this great tool.

Media have evolved. There are so many low-cost options where you can now produce your story. The iPhone has a high-quality camera for photos, video, and audio. Your home computer has an amazing word processor for writing, and for very low cost you can buy publishing software that allows you to put together an informative newsletter. The exciting change is that now you have storage platforms where these video and audio stories can be available.

Most websites and blogsites have very low costs to post your ideas and stories. Not only can you store them in written form, but also in audio and video form. Storage for these video files is less and less expensive and the quality continues to get better.

I spent so much of my career in sales and marketing without learning that storytelling was a better solution than doing business via the telephone.

For most of my career, business came from people who had a lot of context for me, folks with whom I had spent years developing relationships. Context is critical! Either I had coached their kids, or taught them martial arts, or maybe we attended church together. These folks had already seen my character on display in other situations and had no doubt that the person in front of them would deliver on his promises.

They knew Bruce Wayne (without the great wealth) and liked him. But to go from salesperson to superhero, I needed to become Batman, with a whole Bat-belt of media tools.

Video, audio, and written media are the way to convey your story to a much larger audience. It's leverage and it's permanent. It's the answer to the telephone.

We'll talk more about how to execute this idea of building media in Episode 11, but let's first discuss how to get your media in front of your audience—let's discuss distribution.

JUSTICE LEAGUE FORMS A TRIBE

—ᴍ—

Even superheroes need help

*"An A-team of crusaders with a superpowered bench deep enough
to handle any cosmic foe, these heroes are all still very human
at heart, plagued with the flaws that haunt any of us."*

-– DC Comics on the Justice League

BATMAN MET THE GREEN LANTERN for the first time during a crisis. Gotham City was about to be annihilated by a demon from another universe called a Parademon. Together, Green Lantern and Batman pursued and fought the monster that had been sent by Darkseid, the supervillain from the planet Apokolips. Known as the "god of evil," Darkseid ("Darkside") had created an army of demons to attack the human race, conquer Earth and eliminate all free will.

Initially, Batman and Green Lantern did not get along. Green Lantern was disappointed in his fellow crime fighter because Batman didn't have any supernatural powers. Nevertheless, they needed each other to have any chance at success. As they teamed up to fight the Parademon, they unwittingly opened up a sort of Pandora's Box of demons and the two of them could no longer contain the situation. They were losing. They needed help.

So they called some old friends. Friends who could help defend the city; friends who could help advance the cause; the kind of friends we all wish we had—friends with superpowers.

Superman, Aquaman, and Wonder Woman answered the call, but even all those reinforcements could not contain the Parademon army. The Flash and Martian Manhunter also joined the fight. Finally, all together, they began to make progress and ultimately they fought off the Parademon and Darkseid was forced to retreat to his lair.

Although the team won that battle, they knew the war was not yet over. They would need to organize and get ready because they knew this enemy would certainly return... in the next installment of DC Comics.

Together, these superheroes agreed to form the Justice League of America: a group dedicated to fighting Darkseid or any other foe who would threaten peace.

Batman, Superman, and the Green Lantern learned that there comes a time when even a superhero needs a friend. They realized that however strong they were as individuals, they were much more effective as a team. Where one had a weakness, the other had strengths. Working together, they were a formidable force.

Ultimately, you too, will need help. None of us can build a great business on our own. Individually, we are all limited, as there are only so many hours in a day. There comes a time and a place where we need to enlist the help of others. But how?

Once we have carefully crafted a message and a medium with which to share that message, it's time for the next step: distribution. It's time to get the message out where it can be heard, seen, and where it can take root.

You see, a message that nobody hears is pointless. Your business philosophy, your differentiation must be expressed and delivered to the people who can hear it and become believers. These believers, like the Justice League of America, can help your cause and spread your message. They become your distribution points. They bring referrals through relationships. They are your team—your own Justice League of America.

If you agree that relationships are the best way to distribute your messages, then it is your job as a professional to build a following, to engage your audience and to build the tribe. You need people who believe in you and your services so much they are willing to share it with *their* tribe.

Where are these people?

How can you reach them?

How do you get them to become believers?

We will attempt to answer these questions, but first, for context, let's discuss how it's always been done.

Green Lantern and Batman were in trouble and desperately needed help. Batman referred Superman and others to Green Lantern. How did Batman know whom to call? He turned to someone he knew, someone he trusted. So it is with the real estate business. Like Batman, people only refer agents (superheroes) they know and trust.

MY STORY

When I started my real estate business I constantly heard from brokers and trainers that referrals are the key to business. Although that's true, no one had a very good strategy for making this happen.

The first thing they teach you in this business is to build a database. That's very good advice, as you need a list of people who will join your cause. A name, address, phone number, and email address make up your list.

My database was fairly easy to build. I had lots of people through the years with whom I worked, coached, or attended church. I received good advice early on to keep this list clean and to get their permission to add anyone to the list. This permission is huge. It earns the right to make future contact.

The purpose of this database is quite simple: Stay in the heads of your audience. It's hard to earn referrals if folks forget you. You must be top of mind.

My method of building the database was to do the "mayoral campaign" with those folks I already knew. Actually, I still think this is a good idea. Here's how it works:

First, I called each person on my list as if I was running for election to be mayor. I was taught to ask them two questions: 1) Can I add you to my mailing list? 2) If you were going to refer a seller to a real estate agent to sell their home, what agent would you recommend?

The second question really pushed them to identify if they were someone who would actually refer me or if I was just wasting my time engaging them.

What I learned was that many folks already knew an agent and many times it was a family member or close friend. No matter how many times I would contact them, it wasn't likely that I would earn a referral.

With great enthusiasm, I built my list. I called my friends, family, and former associates—just like I was running for mayor. My initial list was maybe fifty people or so.

With that database in place, there were some problems to overcome. How would I engage them? Email, phone or direct mail? What would I send them? How could they refer me if I didn't have a track record? How in the world can someone refer you if they've never seen your work?

You see, even if you are top of mind with your audience, the truth is you can't easily get a referral—even from friends and family—unless they have a good history with you. They might love you, but do they *trust* you? Competency is the key. I'm not sure about you, but I would prefer not to be the surgeon's first brain surgery. OK, so real estate is not brain surgery, but you get my point.

Most of my business in those early days came from the people with whom I had an active relationship. They were people who were already familiar with me and for whom I had demonstrated my character. Such as parents from my daughter's soccer team, fellow church parishioners, and past work associates.

Context is the key. If someone trusts you, even if you have no real estate experience, you have a fighting chance that they will do business with you.

So I sought to engage my audience. Build my tribe.

The rule of thumb was to send something to those on your list once a month. The goal—stay top of mind. But what to send?

"Something of value," my peers would tell me. So I started sending something of value. Refrigerator magnets with my picture and contact info, notepads, pens, football schedules, and recipe cards. You know, *real valuable stuff.*

Years would go by and I wouldn't see much business from my database. Folks who didn't see me regularly didn't have the confidence to send me referrals.

Looking back I now realize my mistake. Everything I was doing was self-serving. Me-focused. My business. What people can do for me. I didn't offer anything for them. I wasn't sharing. I was always asking for a referral, always trying to close the deal—I was always the salesman.

Along with the direct mail items, I was also sending regular emails. My website provider had a system that would send emails on a regular basis to stay in touch. Again, this system was impersonal and self-serving. People knew it was an automated system and probably could tell it was disingenuous. I was just looking to get something from them, not provide something of true value.

You see, the answer to distributing your message in today's distracted world is not refrigerator magnets, pens, hats, and coffee mugs delivered at a booth at the county fair or at a closing table. The answer is that you must first have a message that connects with people and creates a tribe of true believers.

No one taught me to create a message. No one taught me to tell stories to my audience. No one taught me to build a tribe.

So I continued to send monthly recipe cards and did occasional open houses or networking events to build my loose connections and hope to get referrals at some future date. Periodically I would send a thank you card, or do a "pop-by" visit, but it wasn't making a connection. My list was nothing more than a list of people who loosely knew me, but had no real relationship.

Consequently, my business was inconsistent. Some good months, some bad; no real rhythm, and no true growth.

Most real estate agents have no idea where their next transaction will come from. This was my experience. The only way for me to ensure consistency was to continually chase transactions. Open houses. Networking. Telemarketing. Hustling. None of these are relationship building activities. None of them build connection with people, nor do they build a tribe.

You see, a tribe will rally around a set of beliefs. A tribe will rally around a leader who has somewhere to go and something to accomplish. A tribe wants to make a difference.

The key to growing a tribe is to have a unifying message. A belief system. A rallying cry. The message then has to be delivered in story form, over time, consistently.

If your cause and your message are good, they will resonate with those who identify with you. Through these believers you have a better shot at distribution. Through these believers you can change the world.

As discussed in Episode 7, my preferred media are newsletters, blogs, audio recordings in the form of podcasts, and video. Of course, I can't omit the obvious, this book!

A good message, converted to the appropriate media, is now ready for distribution.

THE INTERNET AND ITS POWER

Distribution has never been easier with the advent of Facebook, Instagram, Twitter, YouTube, Pinterest, and countless other social media platforms.

Seth Godin says in his book *Purple Cow*, "Ideas that spread, win." If your cause and your message are good, and you can build a tribe of believers, and if your idea is good, you have a shot at distribution.

We'll discuss in Episode 11 the tactics you can use to distribute media, but the main point I want to get across is that distribution is pointless if it isn't targeted to a very specific audience.

Remember, if you are marketing to everyone, in essence, you are marketing to no one.

Know your audience. A few tips:

* Start by creating an avatar of your ideal customer and map every single decision you make to delight this person. But here's the catch—if you don't genuinely identify with this person then you are not being authentic.
* Authenticity in the social media world is critical to building an audience. Your readers and your listeners will sniff out what is inauthentic and you will lose them forever.
* Distribution in today's environment is nearly impossible without tribe members. You can spend all of the money you want to advertise, but the power of advertising is declining. People are bombarded with ads and are now blocking those ads and ignoring the advertisers.

People want something to believe in. People want to support a cause. People want a leader to follow.

PREFERRED PLATFORMS AND YOUR BEHAVIOR
Distributing your message is about building relationships one person at a time.

You can do this one meeting at a time, or one telephone call at a time. Both of these strategies work, but are ridiculously inefficient. Meetings and phone calls are one-to-one communication. You only have so many hours in a day. What you need is one-to-many communication, where the audience can opt-in. They can choose to engage with you, without being coerced or manipulated into it.

Steve Jobs and Apple, along with the pioneers of the Internet, have provided the answer: Your efforts in distribution should focus primarily on your smartphone.

The preferred platforms at the time of the printing of this book are Facebook, Instagram, YouTube, LinkedIn and Twitter.

Each user consumes the content on these platforms differently and it's important to create your content and your message differently for each channel.

More important than the tactics deployed in each channel is your behavior. Relationship building on social media is no different than it is in day to day life.

People are people. People are not "prospects," "transactions," or "targets."

Too many businesses, and especially real estate agents, are trying to take shortcuts. They ignore every social norm and try to hack the relationship process. Instead of earning trust over time, they deploy sales tactics, scripts, and deception. In their world this makes complete sense, as they have learned in the sales culture that these prospects aren't human beings, they're a transaction.

Relationships were the original distribution method, and relationships are still *the best* distribution method. If you want to win the way Batman and Green Lantern won their battle against an army of demons, you need help. You need a team. You need allies who believe in you and fight at your side.

And to build that team, you need to get the word out about your cause and your mission. Relationships equal distribution. The Internet is the highway. Social platforms are the vehicle.

Let's get that message out. But before you do, make sure you are ready. Because distribution is pointless unless you have a well-designed and remarkable product.

Superman wouldn't fly to join the battle if he did not trust Batman. If your product or services suck, nobody will trust you, so what's the point in distributing your message? Why build that relationship only to have it destroyed by giving your client a horrible experience?

In the real estate business, your product is you and your services.

Let's talk about your product.

WONDER WOMAN HAS A GREAT PRODUCT

—⚭—

The truth and only the truth

"I will fight for those who cannot fight for themselves."

-- WONDER WOMAN

As SHE GREW UP ON an isolated paradise island, Diana had no experience with war. She and her people, the Amazons, had fled the warlike nations many generations ago to establish their own peaceful civilization.

Their tribe of Amazons fled Greece to escape men and their evil deeds. Their civilization of all women set about to create a land of peace— but they also trained as warriors because they knew the outside world was violent, unstable, and at any moment they might have to defend themselves.

During World War II, intelligence officer Steve Trevor's plane crash landed on the island paradise where Diana nursed him back to health.

Because of her incredible fighting skills and her unique talents, she was chosen by her people to travel to America to return Trevor and help end the war. Her mission was to bring love and peace to the world of men, with a specific goal of defeating the Nazis and other forces of evil.

Diana Prince, disguised as a nurse, stayed close to Steve Trevor, mostly to glean intelligence regarding the war. When events warranted, she would spring into action as Wonder Woman.

Wonder Woman's talents were like no other superhero, before or since.

Many publications rate her as the number one superhero of all time. Seeing her at the top of the list was a bit of a surprise to me, but after studying her skills and powers, I have to agree: Wonder Woman may be the greatest superhero of all time. Above all others in the superhero universe, she is the ultimate role model. Our businesses will flourish if we will follow her lead.

First, her mission was the ultimate mission—to bring love and peace. Superman comes close with truth, justice, and the American way, but that does not compare to bringing love to the world.

When mankind returns to the default position of strife and war, her other superpowers come into use. Superhuman speed, the ability to fly, and super strength are all weapons in her arsenal. Of course, she also has tools to go along with these gifts that enhance her effectiveness. Her magic bracelets can deflect bullets, her invisible plane goes undetected by the enemy, and even her tiara can be thrown like a boomerang at great distances. Although these tools and powers are impressive, the abilities and talents that set Wonder Woman apart are the ones not readily seen.

Wonder Woman has an incredible gift of persuasion and is considered the greatest leader. In addition, she can communicate in any language, and can communicate with mental telepathy.

Salespeople and entrepreneurs who harness their communication skills can also become superheroes. Your ability to tell your story and to influence others to action is a skill that can be developed and implemented. Like Wonder Woman, you can solve a lot of problems by improving your communication skills.

Moving people to action, for good or for evil, has been the hallmark of all extraordinary leaders.

Wonder Woman's mission and talents are all based on her integrity. As she fights the Nazis and sets her goals on world peace, she learns that not everyone has this integrity. For this reason she must deploy all of her talents to defend the innocent and punish evildoers.

And the greatest tool in Wonder Woman's tool kit is her "lasso of truth." This golden lasso is unbreakable and infinitely flexible. Those who are wrapped with this magic rope are compelled to tell the truth. The truth is the ultimate weapon. The truth is undefeated. The truth is the core component of a well-designed and remarkable product.

PRODUCTS ARE PROMISES

If you, as an entrepreneur, want to have success and make an impact on the world, you must start with a great product. A great product, like Wonder Woman's golden lasso, starts with the truth.

Products are promises. Your product or service is a promise to the marketplace to solve people's problems. Your product is an extension of your integrity, honesty, and intent.

Great products are built on truth. Great products are well designed. Great products are remarkable.

MY STORY

My product as a real estate agent is my service. My services have been very good over the years, but my service was not well designed nor was it remarkable.

I like to think I have built my services on truth, but a simple trip down memory lane tells another story.

LIAR, LIAR

In Episode 2 I discussed how I used to get phone numbers from unsuspecting prospects. The entire industry was doing it, so I really didn't give it another thought. Tricking someone to make a call to get information only so I could capture their phone number was dishonest. It was taking advantage of someone whom I hoped would do business with me. I bring this up again to ask: Is this the indicator of an honest person? Is this building your services based on truth? The term "call capture" should have been a clue. But I was oblivious, just trying to make a living, and drowning in the sales culture.

This was not the only way I deceived potential clients. "The homeowner would like for you to sign in for security purposes." This was the line I used at my open house events although the homeowners didn't request this in any way. I learned this "tactic" from another agent who found that it increased the number of visitor registrations significantly. The real reason for the registration was that I might convert these visitors into clients. Self-interested. Sales culture.

If those were the only things I was doing that were questionable, maybe I could be forgiven. But as they say on those fast-talking TV ads, "Wait, there's more."

Calls would come in from my online ads and the callers would think I was the listing agent for the property in which they were interested. Instead of disclosing the truth, I would gather the information on the property and try to get them to visit it. The potential clients would assume I knew everything about the house when the truth was I had no clue about the features or any detailed information. Now this may seem minor, but it's a subtle lie, withholding the truth. Remember, this is a "contact sport"—making contact and meeting people is the game. Damn the truth, chase the lead. Sales culture.

Plenty of other misleading statements and tactics could be covered here. Most of them I used, a few I could not. But if we could throw the lasso of truth around the real estate business, agents would admit that real estate—like other sales culture industries—mislead their prospects and clients every single day.

What is really scary to me is that I consider myself a high integrity person. These tactics, as I learned them, didn't seem to be that big of a deal. How is this possible? How could I let some "call capture" company convince me that this was honorable? How could a so-called Christian mislead people?

It is clear to me now why I started to hate my job. So many seemingly small deceptions led me to a path of bigger and bigger deceptions and lies. Truth was not a part of my daily life.

Now don't get me wrong: Once I had a client, I didn't act against their best interests. I am very proud of my behavior with regards to clients. From day one I wanted to be their biggest fan and biggest defender. However, almost all of my marketing and communications with prospects were based on lies and deceit. It's just business. Sales culture.

IMPROVING MY PRODUCT

Later in my career I noticed that in each purchase, my buyers would follow a similar pattern, and I set out to standardize the experience for each client. To improve the process would ensure the quality of my service and enhance their experience.

My job as an agent was to protect clients. I recognized the distinct five phases of a real estate transaction for a buyer and a seller and created binders that walked each client through those phases. As time went by those binders got better and better as I helped clients anticipate what was coming. The binders were great but still were not the answer. In order to provide a great product, I needed my clients to buy in to my system for it to work.

Many clients were just interested in looking at homes and not too concerned about the process. They trusted me to know the process and would not really use their binders. So I stopped using them except for our initial meetings. It was a great way to walk them through the process so that they would have a sense of what was yet to come.

My product was very good, but well designed and remarkable? Not so sure.

I eliminated all of the activities in my business that had any hint of deception. I stopped chasing leads, I stopped doing open houses, and stopped the call capture service so I could get away from those practices. Integrity is the core of my business now, more so than ever, and every day I am implementing new ways to improve my product. The Japanese have a term for it: "kaizen."

Kaizen is a manufacturing philosophy that says your product is never perfect but that you can make continuous improvements to it regularly if you are always open minded to changes that lead to quality.

What I learned through the lasso of truth was that my product, although very good, still had not met the new standard: based in truth, well designed, and remarkable.

So I constantly question the products and services I currently deliver. And you should do the same. I think we can both agree that this component, the product, is the toughest of all the pillars laid out in this book. Most of the products sold on this planet are commodities. You can find real estate companies everywhere. You can find insurance products anywhere. You have endless choices of shoes, clothes, restaurants, and barbers.

My challenge to you, my friend, is to build a product like no other. As an agent, you must figure out exactly how that looks. Your product is *you* and *your* services. Your product is the experience your client has with you. Map it out on paper as it is right now, and then map it out as you would like it to be. The difference between where you want to be and where you are is your homework.

My company is in the process of building the best product we can build that is extraordinary, not just another brick in the wall. This process is never ending as the new standard is "a well-designed and ***remarkable*** product." Just because it's never ending doesn't mean that you can't make dramatic improvements by planning the entire process, beginning to end.

Yes, it is daunting, but totally necessary if you want to live an extraordinary life and make a positive impact in your community.

You see, products that suck will not sustain the relationships that we have built. Remember, those relationships are the cornerstone with regards to becoming a superhero. If your product disappoints those with whom you have built relationships, then those people can't spread the news of your business and ultimately you will fail. Wonder Woman can communicate in any language. So can a good product or service.

But a bad product or service built on lies is not magic bracelets—it's handcuffs holding you back. How can you make an impact if your business begins to die? The truth is, you can't.

Once you have built this product you are ready for the biggest challenge yet. To this point you have been given a roadmap to success—a map that shows you a business with a purpose, with the right person, who tells the right story, that spreads that story, and has an incredible product. That person can win in this game called business and, dare I say, this game called life.

There is however one more obstacle to overcome—the face in the mirror.

Let's talk about you. Let's talk about self-development.

BOY WONDER FINDS SELF-DEVELOPMENT

—⟋ℳ⟍—

Why ask why

"The way we get into these scrapes and get out of them, it's almost as though someone was dreaming up these situations; guiding our destiny."

-- ROBIN, THE BOY WONDER

THE FLYING GRAYSONS WERE A breathtaking spectacle: acrobats performing high-wire, death-defying stunts on the flying trapeze. Their traveling circus act had a very unusual claim to fame: No net.

Make a mistake in this act and there was no second chance.

They were incredibly skilled at their craft, and delighted crowds with their agility and precision. Young Dick Grayson was inspired by his parents as he watched them defy the odds, night after night.

Everything changed for Dick the day he overheard a couple of gangsters threatening the circus. The vile thugs were trying to extort protection money from the owner, but he was having none of it. But the crooks were not to be denied. To show the circus owner that they were deadly serious, they hatched a plan to sabotage the show.

The gangsters applied acid to the trapeze wires before one of the shows and young Grayson's mother and father paid the price as they fell to their deaths.

Crushed, yet angry, Dick Grayson planned to go to the police with what he overheard.

Batman arrived on the scene and informed the boy that the gangsters were working for Tony Zucco, a very powerful crime boss, and if he revealed this knowledge to the police he would most likely end up like his parents. Calmer heads prevailed and Dick relented.

Meanwhile, Bruce Wayne, a billionaire and business leader in Gotham City, decided to take in the young orphan boy. Dick didn't know at the time that Wayne was actually Batman.

Dick set out to avenge his parents' death. While investigating, he again ran into Batman. Working together, they brought Tony Zucco to justice. Along the way, they formed a partnership—and Batman revealed his identity as Bruce Wayne, while he took on the role of mentoring the orphan. Robin, the Boy Wonder, was born.

Being a crime fighter was an easy transition for Robin. Seeing the devastation wrought by criminals on his own family was a huge motivation for Batman's young protege. Robin knew that what he was doing had the potential to save lives and make the world a better place. He realized that if only someone could have intervened, maybe his parents would not have been killed.

Batman took Robin under his bat wing and trained him in the ways of martial arts and investigative techniques. Robin was a natural. His acrobatic training and extraordinary courage were incredible assets, along with his passion to seek out criminals and deliver justice. Talent, combined with passion, is a nearly unstoppable force.

Robin's passion came to him primarily because of a tragic event: He lost his parents, the people most important to him, in a horrific way. This event would drive him to become the best crime fighter he could be. It drove him, under the guidance of his mentor, to amazing self-development.

Like Robin, you can use the experiences in your life as fuel for the fire of self-improvement.

MEANINGFUL SELF-DEVELOPMENT

The year was 1975. It was summer and I found myself at a church in Loveland, Ohio. I don't really remember the specific details surrounding who I was with, but I think it was my Aunt Carolyn who took me. I don't remember any of the sermon, but I distinctly remember the preacher asking at the end of the service if anyone would like to pray to receive Jesus.

As a young boy, I was super sensitive and I knew I wanted to go to heaven, so after the service I approached the man and asked him how I could go to heaven.

He told me I only needed to believe. It was in that moment that I made the decision to follow Christ. Self-development started for me on that summer day when I was 8 years old.

PERFORMANCE-BASED RELATIONSHIPS

It didn't take long for me to decide that to follow Christ, I would have to change some of my behaviors. From that point forward I would spend a lifetime trying to perform, trying to get better. On the surface, this performance mindset, this meaningful self-development mindset, is a good thing. But I had a lot to learn.

You see, I had the idea that self-development would allow me to perform. Perform for God, perform for my boss, perform for my family, perform for others.

When you believe that your performance is the one thing that maintains your relationships, you can become very critical of your own behavior. Constantly questioning myself became a habit. Always aware that my performance could have been better, I developed an incredibly negative inner voice. I was never satisfied.

Performance-based relationships are very dangerous and destructive. In Hollywood, the best example is stage moms; in athletics, you see moms and dads who pressure their kids to perform. Almost always, it ends poorly. The relationship goes something like this: You do this for me, and then I will approve and reward you. If, however, you don't perform the way I expect, then our relationship will suffer.

All my relationships, starting with God, became performance-based. God was my stage mom. I thought I had to earn His love.

My self-development became selfish, in a way. I was improving and getting better to please my "stage mom."

You see, my friend, self-development is not important because it will help you perform for others. No, self-development is important so that you can give away all that you learn and experience and deepen your relationships.

Giving is the way to build relationships. Relationships are all that matters. Relationships over everything.

SELF-DEVELOPMENT WITH PURPOSE

The performance treadmill was getting me nowhere, but it affected everything.

Although I never finished college, my thirst for learning has never subsided. I love learning new things and get really excited about the idea of pushing myself to accomplish something.

Growing my businesses was the easiest way to get me excited. Throughout my career the thing that I most enjoyed was taking a business that wasn't doing well, fixing the fundamentals and seeing growth.

My real estate career has been characterized by chasing one training system after another. Most agents who have had some experience will tell you that the training and development available in the real estate industry is focused on the idea that you must increase your "at bats." It's a numbers game: More contacts equal more opportunities. Leads—everything is focused on leads. Faceless names, email addresses, and phone numbers.

I would sign up for every training course, every sales program, believing that I was working on my craft, investing in myself. Self-development.

Growing your business is laudable. Without a thriving business, you can't care for your family, support your local charity, or impact your community. But lead generation does not build relationships. Focusing only on performance and earning approval is a dead-end.

So, to grow my business, I became a seminar junkie, paying for training courses and sales coaches that were supposed to finally give me a track to run on. I went from one course to the next, chasing, searching for the answers that would finally give me a sustainable business model.

Each seminar brought temporary success, but the tactics and ideas were only designed to increase leads—that were not connected with me in any way. Strangers. However, in my mind I was getting better at my craft, accomplishing something.

I think most entrepreneurs get excited about accomplishing things—taking risks and seeing if they work out. Experimenting. Really, if you think about it, entrepreneurs are like scientists who are fascinated with testing theories and solving problems. Sometimes you solve a problem, sometimes the concoction of chemicals blows up in your face.

My search left me empty. The experiment blew up in the lab. Chasing growth through seminars and sales coaches for all those years left me nothing to give except for sales tactics and short-term lead generation skills. My tank was empty.

Finally, tired of looking outside to seminars and sales coaches for my answer, I took a dramatic step and looked in the opposite direction for my growth. I decided to look inward. I decided that to truly grow, I needed to look in the mirror.

The answer, I decided, was not outside with some coach or trainer.

No, the answer wasn't out there. The answer was inside of me.

TRUE PERSONAL GROWTH

The same thing happened to Robin, the Boy Wonder. He finally came to understand that anger and acrobatic talent weren't enough to make him a superhero. He had to develop his intellect, refine his physical abilities and get control over his emotions to be the best he could be. Our young crimefighter had to overcome himself to realize his dream and become a superhero.

Like Robin, you cannot execute on your talents and passion if you don't first work on the biggest obstacle to success—the face in the mirror.

You are your biggest obstacle. Success begins when you decide to challenge this mightiest of foes.

Self-development began in Episodes 4 and 5 of this book, where we asked two fundamental questions.

1) Why, given my life experiences, do I do what I do?
2) What, given my natural talents, am I designed to do?

Self-development for its own sake is not a powerful enough reason to get started. What's the bigger reason?

You need to be thoroughly convinced that your development is not only for you, but for your broader purpose. The common ingredients for great purposes don't include exotic cars, mansions, and private jets. These things in and of themselves are not wrong, but they won't get you out of bed to get to the gym or give you true satisfaction.

Great purposes include serving others. Real self-development, ironically, is not for yourself, but for your neighbor and for your community.

If we agree that your Big *Why* is going to be the fuel for your self-development, then I think maybe we should take a moment and go back to reexamine the idea: The Big *Why* is your greater purpose. Your reason for being. Your North Star.

The Big *Why* has nothing to do with your occupation. You should not be fooled into believing that your occupation is your identity. I believe that God created you, and He defines you. My prayer is that you would come to believe this as well.

You are in His hands, and He gives us very clear direction about how to find this Big *Why*: ask, seek, and knock. This is covered in the Gospel of Matthew 7: 7.

Shhh. Don't tell anyone. Here's a secret, which by itself is worth the price you paid for this book: All three of those—ask, seek and knock—require *action*.

THE MAGIC INGREDIENT
Dick Grayson took action when he trained as an acrobat. He didn't know it at the time, but this skill would prove invaluable later in his crime fighting career.

You may not know it, either, but action is your current job. It may be boring or frustrating, but if you look closely it has a purpose if *you* have a purpose.

People get confused about their occupations. For some reason, we think that we need to have a passion for the thing that makes us money. This is not true. What is important is that we know *why* we do it. Dry cleaning, truck driving, delivering the mail, selling real estate, none of it is glamorous, but all of it is necessary. All of it is service to our fellow man. All of it is honorable. All of it is action that will lead us to our passion. Asking *why* helps to uncover the underlying reason we do these activities.

Delivering the mail or being an office manager or selling real estate just might be the action you need to take today to grow, to develop your skills, to discover your purpose. Action is the path to passion.

If we discover this passion, then the vehicle with which to carry out the passion becomes less important. The occupation is secondary, not primary. What we *do* in life should not be our focus. All work is honorable. Any business can provide us income or a platform with which to carry out our bigger purpose. Your occupation should not be your entire focus. What really matters is *why* you do what you do.

FILLING UP

Discovering the Five Capitals was a turning point for me. Everything I do now, I do with the goal of building one of these areas of wealth.

The Five Capitals are:

* Financial capital: Money, assets.
* Intellectual capital: Knowledge.

- Physical capital: Health and Energy.
- Relational capital: Relationships.
- Spiritual capital: Inspiration.

Your self-development goals will build one of these five assets. Assets that, once accumulated, can be given away. This is why we must make self-improvement a priority—yes, to gain capital, but more importantly, to give it away to others, to make their lives better, to build meaningful relationships.

These Five Capitals will be your source for operating in life. Each capital matters. Without one of these elements life becomes difficult to operate. You need to be full and overflowing in each category to have any impact on those in your sphere.

As you "fill up" in each capital, you grow in the other capitals. For instance, once your physical capital is grown, then you have energy to grow your intellectual capital, and you can deploy this intellectual capital and affect your financial capital. Giving away financial capital can deepen relationships, completing the circle.

Recognizing the value of the Five Capitals is the beginning. Self-development will come when you dedicate your daily life to build each of these to serve your family, your clients, and your community.

Now that we understand the Five Capitals and their value, it's time to move to the next chapter, it's time to *execute*.

IRON MAN TAKES ACTION

—ɯ—

Don't stand there, *do* something

*"Heroes are made by the paths they choose, not
the powers they are graced with."*

-- IRON MAN

ANTHONY STARK WAS A RICH young man, born to Howard and Maria
Stark, owners of a major electronics and weapons manufacturer, Stark
Industries.

As a boy, he was fascinated with building and controlling machines.
He was so talented that he applied and was accepted to the prestigious
Massachusetts Institute of Technology at the tender age of 15, and grad-
uated with two master's degrees by the age of 19.

Young Anthony went to work for Stark Industries right out of college,
but he was more interested in pursuing a self-centered playboy lifestyle
than focusing on his engineering skills.

His life was forever altered when, at 21 years of age, he lost his parents in an automobile accident.

Anthony became the owner of Stark Industries without a lot of business acumen. Uninterested in running the company, he delegated much of the day-to-day operations to his executive assistant, Virginia "Pepper" Potts.

While attending a field test of military hardware in one of his international plants, Stark and his group were attacked and kidnapped by a gang of terrorists. During the skirmish, he was severely injured by an exploding landmine which left metal shrapnel near his heart.

Whisked away to the kidnappers' camp, Stark found himself in prison, with a cellmate who was a world-renowned physicist, Professor Ho Yinsen.

Wong Chu, the leader of the militant group responsible for the attack and kidnapping, was after something more than simple blackmail. He wanted advanced weaponry for his army. Chu ordered these two world-class scientists to create high-tech weapons for his cause.

Knowing that he couldn't live long with the shrapnel near his heart, Stark conspired with his fellow scientist to develop a battle suit that he could wear. It would use a magnetic field generator to prevent the shrapnel from reaching his heart.

As they worked to finish the battle suit, they were waiting for it to power up when their secret project was discovered by Wong Chu. Professor Yinsen created a diversion to give Stark time to power up the suit, and was killed.

Anthony Stark managed to get into the battle suit of iron and laid waste to the entire lair of Wong Chu in a fit of righteous anger.

Returning home, young Stark redesigned the iron battle suit and created a device that he could wear to protect his heart. Intent on selling the battle suit on the open market, Stark Industries announced it to the public.

That caught the attention of nefarious characters who sought to duplicate the suit for criminal purposes. Made aware of a plot to steal the suit and duplicate it, Stark sprang into action to thwart the criminals. Yet again he donned the suit and defended his creation.

Realizing the implications of selling the suit on the open market changed the young engineer's perspective. He knew he had created an incredibly powerful tool and that the only responsible course of action was to keep the invention in the hands of only one.

He alone would put this awesome power to use as the Iron Man.

Reluctant initially, Anthony Stark became a superhero like any good scientist, through experimentation.

Webster's Dictionary defines the scientific method: *a method of research in which a problem is identified, relevant data are gathered, a hypothesis is formulated from these data, and the hypothesis is empirically tested.*

Hypothesis and theory. Trial and error. Tests, failures and, with perseverance, ultimately success.

Just like Iron Man's story, your journey to success will be paved with these tests and trials. Yes, you must try. Yes, you must fall down. Yes, you must get back up.

Like Iron Man, you must **do**. You must experiment. You must execute.

Now that we have made the case against the sales culture and showed the importance of building relationships, it's time to put our plan into action.

THE JOURNEY

My life and career have been filled with stories of execution, trial and error. I'm not saying it was all success, but what I am saying is that it was a life full of trying.

I could have avoided many mistakes by changing my paradigm. I encourage you to learn from my mistakes and view your endeavor in a new way.

View your business as a journey.

Seeing your business as a journey gives you the appropriate paradigm with which to get started. Begin with a destination, but recognize that you will make countless minor adjustments along the way.

TOOLS FOR THE JOURNEY

Before beginning the execution phase of your journey, it's important first to pack your bags. You know, get the tools and equipment necessary for your adventure. Although embarking on an entrepreneurial mission is a journey, the word "journey" doesn't really do it justice. "Trekking" more accurately portrays what's ahead. According to the dictionary, trekking is *a journey or trip, especially one involving difficulty or hardship.*

Here's the exciting part. Only a few will embrace this hardship. Business is not for sissies. Most of your competitors will not set out on this trek. Most will opt for doing what everyone else does and will settle for businesses and lives that are safe.

Before we start the trek, you will need what I call the Three M's of entrepreneurism. You will need the right *mindset*, the right *mentor*, and the right *mob*.

MINDSET

Our good friend Daredevil provides a mental framework with which to start. He learned from his dad that life is a fight. Entrepreneurs need to gear up for the fight—mentally—every single day.

When you set out, recognize that you are going to get punched. When you are punched you must resolve now that you will regroup and push on. If you get knocked down, you will, like Battlin' Jack Murdock, get back up.

Of all the tools you will pack, none will be more important than your mindset. Get your head right first, and get real about your expectations. Let's discuss some components of proper mindset.

- **The voice.** Your inner voice can be friend or foe. You have a decision to make: Which voice will you give your attention?

In his book *Positive Intelligence,* author Shirzad Chamine identifies two parts of your brain—The Saboteurs and The Sage.

The Saboteurs are a group of ten mindsets that are enemies of The Sage. These voices individually have their own set of beliefs and ideas that are designed to thwart your success. They are negative in nature and they are your enemy.

The Sage, however, is your friend. He will give you calm and inspiration as you face each day. The Sage, like a shepherd, will guide your ways and influence your decision making. He is wise and well aware of your enemies. But there is a catch: You must listen to The Sage. You must give him your full confidence. You must listen to him even when The Saboteurs are at the door and whispering in your ear that you are not good enough, that you are not smart enough, and that you are bound to fail. Deciding to listen to the influences of The Sage is the most important decision before the trek. His guidance and encouragement will be invaluable. I have come to divide my core mindset into two categories—Scarcity mindset and Abundance mindset.

* **Scarcity mindset**. This mindset, at its core, says that there is not enough, that resources are limited. I reject this idea. Scarcity thinking manifests into common wisdom like this pearl we heard from our moms: "Eat all of the food on your plate. People in China are starving." Or, "We have too many people on the planet." Or, "I'd better chase this lead, it might be the only one I get for a while."

This mindset is one of the most dangerous ideas, yet it is the basis of all economic activity. We are constantly bombarded with it and we don't even realize its destructive nature. In essence, this way of thinking is the beginning of worry and anxiety.

It took me years to learn this great truth. Even though I considered myself an optimist, my actions proved that I believed that money was scarce, that health was scarce, that friends were scarce. Inwardly I believed that any day I might see my last client. I operated for most of my career with this poisonous belief system. I believed that our planet was being destroyed and that the world was coming to an end. I believed subconsciously that my business would dry up and die.

The world is not coming to an end; the planet will never be destroyed. Scarcity is a lie. Scarcity lives in the realm of The Saboteurs.

* **Abundance mindset**. The truth is that there is more than enough, and that there will always be more than enough. The universe is limitless. Your talents are infinite.

Most people, nay, *all people*, never reach their full potential. Yet, their potential is so vast we have only begun to scratch the surface of what is possible. Scientists make discoveries daily, yet with each discovery they open a Pandora's box of new questions. The unknowns outnumber the knowns and it's not even close. Look how easy our planet cleans itself, regulates temperatures, provides an overabundance of food and water. The only time there is famine is when men get in the way. The sun effortlessly provides the energy needed for photosynthesis and plant growth. These plants grow free and easy and in overabundance.

Likewise, your business will always have customers and clients. The resources for your success will always be there. You must embrace the abundance mindset and put your faith in a higher power. You must embrace The Sage.

You have a decision to make: Is it The Sage or The Saboteurs? Which voices will receive your attention?

THE NEXT STEP

You are going to need a map on this trek. The good news is that it's already inside you, part of your potential, waiting to be unleashed. I call it:

* **Business religion.** Mindset is guided by your beliefs. It is important to put these beliefs in writing. Beliefs written will help convey your principles to future clients and associates. It will guide your decision making and ensure the path to success is in alignment with your values. Have this document or set of documents in your bag before you set out. It will help to keep you and others on the path to success.

Hustle and hard work alone are not enough. You can hustle and work hard but without a map—your business beliefs—you can end up in the wrong place.

What you *believe* is the most important item in your travel bag. It is your global positioning system, your GPS.

No navigator sets out on a journey without first knowing the destination. The beauty of a GPS is that you can set the destination early and make the hundreds or thousands of minor adjustments to ultimately reach your goal. Your beliefs will illuminate these incremental corrections.

What do *you* believe?

If mindset is foundational and your most important tool, then, to quote the late singer George Michael, "You gotta have faith."

Execution starts with asking—in what, in whom, do you place your faith?

Taking action was never a problem for me. With the heart of an adventurer and full of ideas, I continually take action. But sometimes it costs me. Many of my failures came because I had faith in *me*. The biggest mistakes I have made centered around the idea that I can handle it. Alone.

From a very young age I have been incredibly self-reliant. That trait is applauded in our culture, but depending on your own efforts is not recommended for a successful business or life.

What I've learned is that you cannot do this thing called life alone. You must have *relationships*.

MENTOR
A turning point in my life was sometime around 2006. I had just finished one of my martial arts classes and I saw a familiar face across the room. Doug Feagles, a former customer from the lumberyard, was watching the class. His son Stephen was in my martial arts school and Doug was there to pick up his boy. He waved me over and after a few minutes of catching up, he invited me to have coffee. Intrigued, I agreed to the meeting.

Doug is a high quality custom home builder in my hometown, Loveland, Ohio. Although I knew who he was, I didn't know a lot. The few things

I remember centered around the quality of his homes and the fact that he operated in Loveland. Also, I knew he had a beautiful wife, Sharon, and three beautiful kids. Actually, the reason I even took the meeting was because of my respect for the business that he had built. This guy was a multiple award-winning homebuilder who had participated in almost every home show in Cincinnati—I was honored that he asked. Somehow, I knew that I would benefit much more by our meeting than he would. Looking back—wow, that was such a good decision!

We met at his offices in Loveland and had a great conversation. Our conversation initially was small talk and around business—just catching up.

I was in my fifth year in real estate and was just getting my feet under me and gaining confidence. My wife and I had been chasing our son and daughter around town on soccer fields and basketball courts, and life was chaotic. At the time of our first meeting, I was about to embark on yet another project to make my life even more chaotic.

A very good friend of mine, Barry, ran a charitable organization for inner city youth. Somehow, he and I got together. I was looking for a way to get involved with helping kids. When Doug saw me at the martial arts studio, I was preparing to start a class for self-defense for the kids in Barry's program.

You see, one of the things I have tended toward throughout my life is to overcommit. Although I was a new real estate agent and was striving to grow a client base, I was also trying to give back. The problem was that my calendar was already full. Not only did I have a son and daughter in high school who were very active, but I was trying to do too much. My intentions were good, but as usual I was overcommitting.

During our first coffee meeting, I think Doug sensed my chaotic lifestyle. What I first noticed about him was his sense of calm. He wasn't running nearly as hard as me, but here was a very successful guy in his own right. Something about him was different.

You see, in the world of the sales culture it was a badge of honor to be busy. If you weren't living a chaotic life, then you just weren't hustling enough. I was naive. I thought what I was doing would lead to success because I was crazy busy. This is good, right?

Well, it seems as if Doug had another motive for inviting me to coffee. Doug was looking for men to mentor. Doug is a Christian and he was searching for someone with whom he could build a relationship.

Our single meeting turned into a regular appointment on my calendar at 6:00 a.m. every Friday. At first we met just to encourage one another regarding business and life, but it morphed into so much more.

Turns out, Doug is a member of Christian Businessmen's Connection (CBMC), a national and international organization dedicated to sharing the message of Christ in the business community. The goal of the group is to build relationships with businessmen. Long-term relationships. Life-long relationships.

Why? Because relationships are the only way to get context for another human being. It takes time to hear someone's story, to understand their background and their struggles. Trust is not earned in a five-minute conversation, so time is a key element in any relationship. Doug and I put in the time. I began to understand that CBMC was a movement of men who wanted to change the world, one relationship at a time.

Friday, after Friday, after Friday, this man built into me. We discussed God's plan and will in my life and it wasn't long before I began to understand my life was out of control.

You see, Doug had this peace about him. He had control over his calendar and would not let the outside world dictate his schedule. Doug didn't tell me my life was out of control, Doug just lived his life and by watching him I knew something was wrong.

Doug introduced me to other men in the organization. Men whose guidance and influence began to shape my worldview. Men like Mike Marker, the patriarch of our group in Cincinnati.

Mike, like Doug, also exhibited this peace about him that I so desperately wanted. Although he was meeting with multiple men and building into those relationships, I never got the sense that Mike was in a hurry. He had this carefree spirit about him, almost like a great shortstop who makes his craft look so easy. You know, a guy who has it all under control even though a runner is barreling down on him with spikes flying high. Unflinching, calm, collected, seemingly effortless.

Mike is a local developer who has been a leader as an entrepreneur as well as a leader in the Christian community. His background has given him the credibility with businessmen that is needed to develop these relationships. You see, I have learned from Mike and Doug that whatever your occupation, you have an opportunity to build relationships with those people who populate your given industry or community. In other words, you can make an impact right where you are; you don't have to travel great distances to Africa or South America.

So, back to my martial arts training for at-risk kids. Those kids were in downtown Cincinnati, twenty miles from my house in a different community, and my schedule was already too crowded. I learned through CBMC that I could make a bigger impact by staying in my lane and looking to give back, right where I was—in the business community.

I decided against the self-defense classes for kids and focused on first learning (filling up) and giving back in a different way, by building into my own relationships.

MOB

Okay, "mob" is not the perfect word, but how can you have the three M's with the word team? Work with me here.

Our initial meeting turned into a ten-year relationship where Doug built into me. We laughed, we cried, we learned about God's will for our lives. Along the way, my relationships grew with other guys in the group such as Si, Bob, Scott, Darren, Dave, Josh, Steve, Steve W., Tim, Dan and many others. All of these guys, all of these relationships, helped me to grow as a person, so that one day I could do the same for another.

These men, all businessmen, were willing and open to sharing their lives. Your business growth will also come from those around you who are willing to share their experiences. Shared lessons from both successes and failures are valuable, and will help you coordinate your journey.

Our mob (team) gathered around a set of beliefs. Our religion. Not just the Christian faith, but the core beliefs of CBMC—building into one-on-one relationships to experience life together, and use those relationships to affect the wives and children of each man; also to affect the brothers, sisters, mothers, fathers, business partners, associates... You get the picture: One life touches so many people, and if that life is following the ultimate Shepherd, the impact is exponential.

Like any successful organization, you must build your team, your tribe, around a set of beliefs, your business religion. Effectiveness can only be achieved if all your associates are pulling in the same direction.

In the back of this book is a list of principles that are at the core of Bastion REALTORS®. Hopefully, by reviewing this list, you will see some of the principles that guide my every decision, and be inspired to create a list of your own.

Sharing your beliefs will attract like-minded people who want to help you achieve your mission. These people will become your tribe, your team, your mob.

RELIGION VS. TACTICS

Tactics come and tactics go. What works today might not work tomorrow, but principles are timeless. Your business religion should be built on these principles and not on short-term tactics.

Like CBMC, or any great organization, you must carefully choose your business religion. Think it through, ask your teammates, and build your business on principles.

Now that we have our travel bag packed with the right tools and equipment, let's get started. It's go time. It's do time. It's time to execute.

The following pages will give you some tactics that you can use to implement your purpose-driven business. Use these checklists to get your business going in the right direction, but remember that the tactics and tools will change over time.

I encourage you to focus on these principles and you will build a business that will stand the test of time.

Knowledge without application is pointless, and faith without works is dead. Action, my friend, is the foundation to all success.

Let's get started. The following pages will help you to act on the following:

1) Find your Purpose
2) Tell your Story
3) Execute your Mission

FIND YOUR WHY

—⁓—

STEP ONE: TRACE YOUR CAREER path and write down your education-al experiences, your job history, and volunteer experiences. At this point focus only on your job titles, dates, and responsibilities.

Your experiences are the place to begin to find meaning. Many times the things for which we care the most are things we do for free. Did you volunteer at a homeless shelter? Did you volunteer at a hospital or senior care facility? Did you help at the animal rescue facility? Did a relative or a close friend suffer loss?

In my case, I have always been an entrepreneur and knew that I wanted to grow a business. What I didn't know was how to do that and fulfill my bigger purpose.

My defining moment came over time. As a Christian, I wanted to share God's goodness with people in my sphere, so I knew that element would be the biggest part of my purpose.

The question became how do I combine my ambition to build a great business with the greater purpose of introducing people to Christ? By writing down my job history, coaching experience, management experience, the answer started to reveal itself.

Step Two: Ask, Seek, Knock (Matthew 7:7). For those of you who do not have a lot of experience, or maybe have never volunteered, it's time to experiment. Go. Do. Try. The faster you find out what you don't want to do, the quicker you will discover your purpose.

Don't be confused, we are not talking about your gifts and talents just yet. What injustice in the world would you like to correct? What cause lights your fire?

In my case it was my chaotic childhood that held the answer. My fire gets lit when I see a child neglected or trapped in poverty and despair. I want kids to get good parenting, and to be fed, and to be educated. I understand this subject better than most, and if you want to get me fired up then try to tell me that government is the answer to poverty. You'll get my unapologetic wrath regarding the damage done to me growing up in the welfare culture.

To me, a job is the greatest welfare program. Therefore, entrepreneurs are my heroes. They are gutsy enough to take risks to start a business and grind it out every day with all of the naysayers and backbenchers telling them they can't. Entrepreneurs and business owners provide jobs for people who in turn keep their families fed. Families are blessed by the ambition of the entrepreneur.

I share this to illustrate why it's important to know your purpose. Mine is to defend the defenseless by using my business to support charities that align with my greater purpose.

How about you? What lights your fire? Figure this out and marry it to your occupation, whatever the occupation.

Step Three: Read. Listen. Watch.

Growing your intellect and finding answers in life requires listening. You can listen to wisdom by reading books, listening to podcasts, and watching videos.

The internet has changed the world. You can get most answers by a simple search. Take action to learn about subjects that might give you guidance as to your purpose. Ask. Seek. Knock.

Suggested Books

Start with Why – Simon Sinek
The Purpose Drive Life – Rick Warren
The Power of Right Believing – Joseph Prince
The E-Myth – Michael Gerber
Loving Monday – John Beckett
The Invested Life – Joel C. Rosenberg & Dr. T.E. Koshy
Awaken The Giant Within – Tony Robbins
Choose Yourself – James Altucher

Suggested Podcasts

Gary Vaynerchuk – *The GaryVee Audio Experience*
Joseph Prince – *Joseph Prince Audio Podcast*
James Altucher – *The James Altucher Show*
Ron Adams – Loveland Advice Givers

Suggested YouTube Channels

Tedx Talks
Gary Vaynerchuk
Casey Neistat
Ron Adams – Bastion Daily

TELL YOUR STORY

—ᵐ—

STEP ONE: IN ORDER TO tell your story, you must first determine: What are your talents? What are your skills? What is your Big Why?

I lied to myself for many years. I did not face the truth of my skillsets or the truth of my talents. Actually, I never considered it. But here's the deal: Before you do a self-audit you have to agree that whatever the truth, you will accept it. If you are pursuing a career that doesn't fit your skillsets or talents, you must agree to modify and correct your course. The truth is the truth. If you aren't good at interpersonal communications I can save you some time: Real estate sales is not for you. But maybe real estate support is a better fit.

Before you tell your story you need to know yourself. Where are you on the hero's journey?

Step Two: It's Time for a Self-Audit.

- Ask your family, friends, and associates this question: What do you think are my strengths? Write them all down. Make sure they understand you need the unvarnished truth.

* Write down all your passions. Both positive and negative. This exercise will give you clarity. This exercise will reveal the real you.
* Pray. Ask God, "What is the purpose for which I am designed?"
* Look over the education and skills list we did in Find Your Why, and compare it to this new list. The combination of the two lists will reveal some truth.

Step Three: Write Your Origin Story.

* Follow the "hero's journey" roadmap: 1: The Ordinary World and the Call to Adventure. 2: Meeting the Mentor and the Refusal of the Call. 3: Approaching the Dragon's Den and Seizing the Treasure. 4: The Road Back, Resurrection, and Return.
* Once written, your story can be used to tell the world what you and your business are purposed to do. This story becomes a part of you and becomes committed to your memory. This story is the foundation for writing the script of your life. Commit to the journey.
* Become a student of storytelling, realizing that this is a skill you will need to practice in order to be effective (remember, it's a journey).

Step Four: Create Your Message.

Knowing your origin story comes in handy when you meet a new client. The idea is to send the origin story in writing before your first meaningful meeting with a client so that they have context. Along with the origin story you will also send a document that explains how your business is different.

Differentiation is critical for your business. If you can't tell someone how you are different, then you are just another agent, a commodity. Commodities are traded on the open market and the lowest price wins.

Your origin story, combined with your unique approach to business (how you are different), are the two elements that set you apart from all other competitors. If this story is compelling, and if you can communicate value, the client will pay your price. This becomes your message, your mission.

If your story is not good, or it is not authentic, then you might as well just lower your price and become the low-price leader in your market. Save yourself the time and trouble and just be like everyone else.

To tell or not to tell your story—that is the question. Both decisions are painful. One has short-term pain upfront, because crafting an authentic story is difficult; but the other path, choosing not to, has pain in the end, as illustrated in this book.

Once your message is dialed in, it's time to move forward.

Step Five: Spread Your Message.

Commit your story to media:

- Create a blog site and publish your story
- Create a video version
- Create a newsletter version
- Create an audio recording
- Write a book or an e-book that tells your story

Create your client avatar: What are the demographics of your ideal client? Whom do you want to serve? Where do they live? What car do they drive? What's their income? Profession? Where do they shop?

All your distribution efforts should be filtered through this ideal client. All your marketing should be directed to your avatar. Be intentional.

Distribute your Media:

* Commit to learning the social media platforms and distribute your stories
* Facebook, Instagram, Snapchat, LinkedIn, Pinterest, YouTube, Podcasts are all viable storytelling platforms
* Begin telling these stories in all platforms that are native to your targeted audience
* Create a weekly email to your audience—a story based around your character
* Send monthly newsletters to your audience—a story based around your message
* Start a daily YouTube show—documenting your daily travails
* Start a podcast—have guests who match your avatar
* Start blogging daily—attracting your avatar

Suggested Books

The E Myth Revisited – Michael Gerber
The War of Art – Steven Pressfield
Wired for Story – Lisa Cron
Winning the Story Wars – Jonah Sachs
Mastering The Craft of Writing – Stephen Wilbers
The Storyteller's Secret – Carmine Gallo

Suggested YouTube Shows

Gary Vaynerchuk
Casey Neistat

EXECUTE YOUR MISSION

—ᴍ—

STEP ONE: REVIEW THE QUALITY of your product.

Without a great product or service, none of this relationship advice will work. How can your relationships be strong if you give horrible service? How will your story be virally spread if the product doesn't perform? The answer is, it can't.

Relationship building only works if you keep your promises. Your products and services promise to solve a client's problem. If the product fails, the relationship fails.

Sales processes should be managed much like the manufacturing world. William Edward Deming brought back to American manufacturing the idea of continuous improvement from the Japanese companies where he helped produce much higher finished quality. The Japanese call it "kaizen" which means continual improvement. Your product in the real estate business is you and your service. And like any product, your product must get better. Here's how:

- Review your product and services and document the processes
- Measure the quality of the product regularly

- Set up regular meetings to review the results of the measurements
- Make regular changes to your processes going forward, forever

Step Two: Self-development.

Intellectual capital

Your education and skills should be a priority for the rest of your career. In business, as in life, there are only two options. 1) you are learning and growing or 2) you are dying.

This is binary. It's true of businesses and it's true of people in their personal lives as well. There is no such thing as staying the course or coasting.

Massive change is underway as technology is creating disruptive forces that will impact every business. Those who continue to learn and who are willing to work will be positioned to take advantage. Those who don't will pay the price.

Time, the premium asset

When you talk about self-development, the first obstacle for people and the most common excuse is, "I don't have the time."

Let's talk about time.

Time needs to be traded for whatever you want in life. Want to get healthy? Put in thirty minutes at the gym. Want money? Forty hours a week at your job. Want intellect? Commit to hours of study and, of course, tuition. You get my point.

If time is the premium asset, then your calendar is the most precious tool.

Your calendar is the beginning of self-development. You have to prioritize your time. Or better yet, leverage your time.

To leverage your time, you need a few tools.

* iPhone or Android
* Earbuds
* Podcasts or audiobooks

I can't think of a better way to leverage your time. Listening to podcasts or audiobooks while driving, exercising, or doing work around the house is the perfect opportunity to increase your intellectual capital. You can take a one-hour exercise routine and magically turn one hour into two. Time to do laundry? Time to mow the lawn? More podcasts or digital audio books allow time travel. Twenty-four hours a day can become twenty-seven hours a day!

Never before in history have we had access to these kinds of tools and this kind of content. Books, e-courses and seminars are also great ways to grow. Reading, along with consuming content via audio and video, can help you improve your writing skills, your marketing skills, and your interpersonal skills. These skills will increase your ability to earn and improve your financial capital.

Protecting my time has been an obsession of mine for the past few years. No more networking events. Instead I've focused on storytelling and writing skills. No more open houses. Instead I've focused on getting rest for the week so I might have more energy to focus on my clients. No more basketball. What? Okay, this was a little over the top, but I did not see a basketball game this entire year and most of last year, and I am a huge fan, My point with all of this is that you must prioritize your time. If you want to live a life worth living, you must first improve your intellectual capital and become more valuable to your clients and customers.

Here's the cool thing about eliminating ninety minutes of basketball. Now you can add ninety minutes of reading or listening. I call it Jiu-Jitsu—taking a negative and turning it to a positive. Your calendar today has lots of opportunities for you to start making change.

Physical health

Great relationships are difficult to sustain if you are not healthy. Make your physical health a top priority.

Your schedule and your checkbook are a direct reflection on what is important to you. Think of the checkbook and calendar as a mirror. Hold up your checkbook registry and your calendar right now. How much time and money do you spend on your health? Where on your calendar is your health represented? Where in your checkbook registry is your health represented? Does the local bar or restaurant get represented in your checkbook log, but not a gym membership?

Show me your calendar, show me your checkbook log, and I'll show you what you value.

* Schedule one hour a day for your exercise (thirty minutes minimum)
* Keep that appointment

- Schedule your meals
- Keep that appointment
- Win at the grocery store—don't bring it home if it won't help you win

Here's the deal. We all know that our diet is the most important component of health, yet we ignore this most important appointment. Put your diet on your calendar and keep the appointment. For me, I have exercise first thing in the morning for me to win. My wife is a huge help for me regarding diet, as she only brings home groceries that contribute to health. You know the rules: no sugar, low carbs. Seriously, Google this subject and you will find out what to do. My encouragement to you is to just schedule diet and exercise on your calendar.

Spiritual health

Spiritual health is more important than physical health and intellectual health, but for practical reasons I've listed it last.

Mindset is the most important ingredient to your success. What you believe will manifest itself, so you must get your mind right.

- Be diligent about what you watch, hear, and read
- Eliminating the negatives is the first step to success

News is negative. Most television is negative. Many people are negative. These influences are toxic. I eliminated cable news television from my life and my outlook on life got much more positive. Horror movies, most radio shows, and much of social media are negative. This impacts your mind as you subconsciously absorb these messages. Protect your mind by filtering what you consume.

A mental Jiu-Jitsu move is to replace those negative influences with positive ones. Examples are soothing music, positive podcasts, inspiring movies, books, or television shows.

A higher calling

Everyone has a different opinion and approach to this subject. My personal relationship with Jesus Christ is the foundation for everything in my life. You may not have the same opinion, and I respect that. However, I am convinced that Christ is the answer to all questions spiritual or otherwise.

For the purposes of self-development, I encourage you to go on a journey and ask the tough questions regarding your spiritual health. It is so difficult to accomplish your life goals if you don't have hope. Hope, as my good friend Doug reminds me, is Jesus.

Suggested Books

Rework – Jason Fried & David Heinemeier Hanson
The Dip – Seth Godin
The Obstacle is the Way – Ryan Holiday
The Power of Right Believing – Joseph Prince
The Bulletproof Diet – Dave Asprey
Ego is the Enemy – Ryan Holiday
The Rise of Superman – Steven Kotler
Deep Work – Cal Newport

Tools of Titans – Tim Ferriss
Tribes – Seth Godin
The 4 Hour Work Week – Tim Ferriss
How to Fail at Almost Anything and Still Win Big – Scott Adams
Influence – The Psychology of Persuasion – Robert Cialdini
The Power of Positive Thinking – Norman Vincent Peale

BASTION BELIEFS

—m—

* We are Protectors
* We are Loyal
* We are Charitable
* We are Authentic
* We are Positive Thinkers
* We encourage Holistic Self-Development
* We are a People Business

Protectors: Our primary job is to protect. This is the definition of the word "Bastion." We view this as our highest calling. There are times to fight for a cause, and we are always learning to be better defenders. Our own interests come second to the interests of our clients.

Loyalty: Our fellow Bastion agents are fellow warriors. We stand by them, and they are not our competition. We help each other without expectation of compensation. We share what we learn with one another. Every voice is heard and is important. It is management's goal to hire only positive associates. In the rare case of a negative influence, out company vows to protect our culture and address such individuals swiftly.

Charity: Another word for this is "love." Our business exists to do good for our neighbors. Our efforts produce profits, which go to care for our families and our neighbors. Giving is a natural extension of love. Our company donates to charity with each transaction. We will not promote this in our public advertising. However, we do share it with our clients and future clients privately, because it is important that they see this in practice to encourage them to do the same. Giving is the secret to personal happiness and prosperity, but it applies to a corporation as well. This giving does not come from an agent's commission. Forced giving is not giving, it is compulsory and of no value.

Authenticity: You can be *you*. We don't want you to do or be something phony that makes you uncomfortable. We want you to pursue self-discovery, to find your passions and talents and to put them to work for greater good. We want each agent to live a fulfilling life and to make a difference in others' lives as well. If you are true to you, you can be satisfied that you are contributing in the right way. Don't be pretentious, don't be fake. Keep it real. The real you is more than good enough. We believe in One Life—that we are the same real person at work, at play, or in public, naturally incorporating all aspects of our life in all that we do.

Think positive: We expect that good things are going to happen. We have a confident expectation of good. We believe that success, like gravity, is certain and dependable. We recognize that the things that come out of our mouths have both positive and negative impacts on us and on those around us. We understand the importance of each word and its power. Words are not just thrown around, but are harnessed for their power to do good. To our best ability, we eliminate negativity, negative words, and harmful jokes. However, we still have fun. Each day is an adventure and we expect it to be fun and exciting. Prosperity comes to us because we expect it. Our success is measured by positive results not the dollars made from a sale. We don't stress or panic; we are calm and patient. We believe in *Kaizen*, the principle of continual improvement.

Holistic personal development: Our company believes in training the full person. We take into consideration the entire Five Capitals: Spiritual, Physical, Relational, Intellectual, and Financial. It is our goal to train and encourage our team members in all of them. Each agent should strive to grow and fill up in these five areas, to make greater impact in their families and in their community. Great agents, who are healthy, happy, knowledgeable, comfortable and in the right positive mindset are more successful serving their clients.

People: We are not in the real estate business. We are in the people business. We keep our clients' interests in the top of our minds. We look for ways to assist them that sometimes go beyond a transaction. We look to encourage them and be their greatest cheerleaders and fiercest defenders. We also recognize that not every client or agent is the right fit for our Bastion philosophy. But we welcome agents and employees from all religious and ethnic backgrounds, so our company can reflect our marketplace and represent the diverse needs of our clients. We are a *relationship* culture, not a sales culture, so we don't use or allow cold calling, door knocking, or other "transactional" strategies. Our aim is to build lasting relationships. That is our brand and our mission.

—ɰ—

***Start With Why,* Simon Sinek (Penguin, 2009).** This book covers the big idea of what the author calls the "Golden Circle," a simple diagram that encourages you to first focus on "*Why*." It will lead to a better how and a better what. The Golden Circle is a model of what mathematicians, architects, musicians and artists call the Golden Ratio. This Golden Ratio shows up in great art, music, astronomy, and throughout nature. The Golden Circle and the question *Why* should be the first and most carefully considered question of every endeavor. Your *Why* will get you through the difficulties that always arise when you set your mind to any accomplishment. This book should be on your shelf. It's a must for every leader of any organization or future leader. This book will guide you to look in the mirror and question who you are and why you get out of bed. It will encourage you to answer the question, "Why would anyone care?" And your Why will give you the fuel for your what. *Start With Why* is a fundamental book for any aspiring achiever.

***The Dip,* Seth Godin (Portfolio, 2007).** Seth Godin might be my favorite writer. He is efficient with his words. This book is only 76 pages long, so you should be able to read this in a day or two. The book focuses on three curves: The Dip, The Cul-de-Sac, and the Cliff. The Dip is the curve that leads to success; the other two curves ultimately lead to failure. All three curves are represented by the typical Cartesian Plane, represented by your typical business graph. The Dip is the only curve we must focus on to be ultimately successful. The idea is that a Cul-de-Sac (French for dead end), goes nowhere so is ultimately not worth pursuing. Examples might be a dead-end job, or a commoditized industry where your product is only another "me too" product. The Dip on the X axis is represented by RESULTS: the Y axis is EFFORT. Every project worth doing has a major dip right before major success. An example might be the goal of writing a book. In the beginning, you are enthused and highly motivated and the words come easy. Then you have ideas that might not be easy to transition, and you get stuck. It's a grind but you don't quit, because you know that on the other side will be success. You just have to get through the Dip. If Seth Godin writes it, and you are at all interested in writing, business, or self–development, you must buy it.

The E-Myth, **Michael Gerber (Ballinger, 1988).** This is a MUST-own book for all aspiring entrepreneurs. It follows the story of Sarah, a pie maker who likes to make pies so much, she decides to open her own business, a lifelong dream. She quickly realizes she is great at making pies, but doesn't know much about how to manage a business or to organize it to serve her, as opposed to her serving it. The book defines the MYTH of being an Entrepreneur, the "E Myth." The truth is, most business owners are NOT entrepreneurs but instead technicians, such as pie makers, mechanics, and doctors. However, they are NOT entrepreneurs. That is a different skill set altogether. Each business should have three leaders: 1) entrepreneur, 2) manager, and 3) technician. This book describes the evolution of technicians to true entrepreneurs by way of working ON their business, and not IN their business. The author also encourages you to develop your prototype business, as if you were going to duplicate it multiple times, maybe in other markets.

He calls this the TURN KEY revolution—like Subway or McDonald's franchises. The characteristic that makes this book valuable is this: The author challenges you to ask the questions: Who do you want to be? What kind of life do you want to live? What do you value most? Those questions help you discover your PRIMARY AIM. That discovery alone would make the book a great value, but it has the added bonus of showing you how to transform your PRIMARY AIM to an overall systems strategy that covers organizational, management, people, and marketing strategies.

The War of Art, **Steven Pressfield (Black Irish Entertainment, 2011).** This book helps you to recognize the unseen force that prevents you from sticking to your diet plan, stops you from starting that business, and foils your best attempts to finish that painting. The author calls this invisible enemy RESISTANCE. It shows up every single day, in every single circumstance when you are trying to accomplish any worthy goal. The author arms you with the tools you need to deal with this enemy and how to defeat it. He calls this method "Turning Pro." My interpretation of this term is "put on your big boy pants." Resistance is not a quitter. It meets you at every turn and you need to get mentally prepared for it. The highlight of the book, for me, was the author's recognition that we need a higher help, which he calls "angels in the abstract." I would call it spiritual inspiration or God's hand. These angels work on your behalf to do battle with the resistance and aid you in your quest. The book is written to encourage writers, but is applicable to anyone who is trying to "do" something. It addresses fears, faith, taking action, and being true to yourself. This book belongs on your bookshelf. It is an easy read at only 165 pages, and could be read in a weekend easily as many chapters are only a page or two. If you are just getting started with writing as your goal, this would be the perfect book with which to begin.

Rework, **Jason Fried & David Heinemeier Hannson (Crown Business, 2010).** This is one of the best books on business I have ever read. It is concise, to the point, full of practical advice. Where to begin? I could write a three-page review and it might not be enough, so here goes: First, here are the MYTHS that *Rework* punches in the nose: 1) learning from mistakes is overrated; 2) planning is guessing; 3) workaholics are NOT HEROES!; 4) enough with entrepreneurs! Start a business; not a startup; 5) outside money is a bad idea; 6) build half a product; 7) ignore the details; 8) meetings are toxic; 9) say no by default; 10) DON'T write it down. Honestly, I could list thirty or forty takeaways from this book. It is 268 pages, but that is deceptive. The chapters are written with such simplicity and efficiency many of them are only one page or two. The only reason it takes a while to read is that the content is so rich you will find yourself wanting to take notes. My biggest takeaway is this: If you don't have this book in your library you are cheating yourself. Keep it close and refer to it regularly as it will remind you what is important, which to me is the overarching theme: What is important? What should be ignored?

Choose Yourself, **James Altucher (CreateSpace, 2013).** This is an interesting book that exposes the current state of the economy and your place in it. The author makes the point that you no longer need to wait for someone to "pick you." We have all experienced that time as a kid where you were the last one picked for the team. Remember how upset you were because someone did not choose you? Now the world has changed. The time where you needed a corporation to choose you is over. You have access to all the tools needed to choose yourself, make your own way, create your own product. It is easier than ever to get a product made or create a service, and then build it, market it, and sell it. ALL ON YOUR OWN! The Internet has flattened the world and we are never going back. The premise of the book is that even though you have a job and work forty hours, you don't have to wait for that promotion. Instead, start a business on the side. Grow your audience and build that thing inside of you that taps into your creativity and allows you to plot your freedom, both financially and spiritually. One of the primary takeaways from the book is that you have four bodies that need to be healthy in order for you to succeed—physical, emotional, mental, and spiritual. You can be healthy in all these bodies by implementing what he calls the Daily Practice, which are specific tasks. Once you are practicing good habits and you are healthy in all areas, you will perform at a high level and become someone worth following. The big takeaway: You can empower yourself to make your mark if you *Choose Yourself.*

Ego is the Enemy, **Ryan Holiday (Penguin, 2016).** Holiday is an interesting writer. His vocabulary is well beyond mine and I need a dictionary by my side when reading his books. He is brilliant and has a passion for history, which comes to light in this book. The book is divided into three sections: 1) Aspire; 2) Success; 3) Failure. Holiday explores the idea that you, more specifically, your ego, is your enemy. Woven throughout the book are stories of General William Tecumseh Sherman, a Civil War general who along with Ulysses S. Grant helped win the war for the Union Army. Sherman was not someone who sought the spotlight and was quite comfortable just doing his job and accomplishing the work at hand, not seeking credit or the spotlight. Juxtaposed to Sherman's attitude is General U.S. Grant, to show how each man's ego, or lack thereof, shaped their destinies. Much of the philosophy shared in the book emanates from ancient Stoic Philosophy, which was practiced by thinkers such as Seneca and Roman Emperor Marcus Aurelius. The highlight of the book is the "What's Important to You" chapter (page 114), where Holiday introduces the word *euthymia,* a Greek word that means to take your own path, and to stay away from the distractions along the way that take you away from your goal. The author gives many real-life stories and examples of how dealing with ego has affected many in different walks of life, including sports, business, and politics. The main point of the book is to check your ego at the door. Like Steven Pressfield's revelation about resistance, Holiday has introduced me to another enemy, and this one looks back from the mirror each day. The book is small, and good to pack in your briefcase, but don't let the size fool you. It took me a solid week and a half to get through so much valuable content. Everyone can benefit from this book. It belongs on your bookshelf.

#AskGaryVee, Gary Vaynerchuk (HarperBusiness, 2016). This is a practical book based on Gary's very popular YouTube show by the same name. You ask questions, he gives answers. It's great for marketers and business owners. I view it as more of a reference book than anything else. It opened my eyes to the value of social media and to advertising and storytelling in general. What is amazing to me about Gary is his business instincts. A self-described D and F student who hates to read, Gary is incredibly insightful. His favorite topics, and the ones that make the book worthy of your bookcase are these: 1) Self-awareness. Gary makes the claim, and I wholeheartedly agree, that you need to know yourself, BE REAL with yourself. If you are 5'9" and 175 pounds you cannot expect to be an NBA player, it's just not your natural talent. Well, what is? Identify that talent and go ALL IN on your gifts. Stop trying to fix your weaknesses and deploy your own personal talents and abilities. Stop trying to be someone else. Be you. 2) Give, Give, Give, then Ask. This is also a biblical principle and seems to be more evident to me as I live my life. Financial health, physical health, relationship health, intellectual health and spiritual health all point back to this one principle. Give. Don't be a taker, but be a giver. 3) You need to realize that if you are in business, you should be a MEDIA company. Someone with a message. If you are in business, you need to have a business religion, an overall message, and you need to share that message with an audience that can support your cause. This guy is off the charts with his EQ (emotional quotient or emotional intelligence), and is one of the great communicators of our time. Buy this book.

Influence: The Psychology of Persuasion, **Dr. Robert Cialdini (HarperBusiness, 2006).** I was introduced to Dr. Robert Cialdini's writings by a marketing expert who mentioned the role of psychology in the marketing of businesses. It got me to thinking about my sales and management career and the number of books I have read on the subject. How does psychology play a role in my current job? Why do people do what they do? Outside of a few psychology classes in college, my studies have been limited. As I searched for authorities on the subject, I kept hearing this author, and this book specifically. The book introduces the six "weapons of influence." They are: Reciprocation, Commitment and Consistency, Social Proof, Liking, Authority, and Scarcity. Reciprocation is invoked when one person gives something. The receiver feels compelled to give back in some way. Salespeople use this weapon regularly—free samples at the grocery or a complementary magazine subscription. Commitment and Consistency is more subtle. Someone tries to influence you to do something so they get you to commit to your beliefs and then convince you that to be consistent with those beliefs, you must buy their product or vote their way. Social proof happens when someone perceives you well because of your associations. If you are hanging out with other important people your credibility increases. Liking is the most obvious of influencers. You will more readily be influenced by someone you like, someone with whom you identify. Authority is an interesting influencer. Someone who has authority on a subject, or who portrays an air of authority, has the ability to influence in certain circumstances. A doctor, an author, a police officer, all have the ability to influence because of their perceived authority. Scarcity is also a powerful influencer. If something is perceived as rare or limited, it has a higher perceived value. Companies regularly use scarcity to influence behavior. For instance, McDonald's offers the McRib for a "limited time" to attract customers. Mattel introduces limited edition Barbie Dolls to drive sales. The beauty of this book is that it gives you a glimpse into the behavior of your fellow man and a look in the mirror as you are made aware of how the world tries to influence you. Bonus references from the 1980s make this bookshelf worthy.

***The Rise of Superman*, Steven Kotler (Amazon Publishing, 2014).** I wanted to know more about the subject of flow. Specifically, I wanted to know how I could grow as a person and how to fit it all into my schedule. I started the search and came across this book. It turns out the author has studied this subject for over a decade and assembled a number of stories of superhuman feats based around the accomplishments of extreme sports athletes. People such as Danny Way, who jumped over the Great Wall of China on a skateboard; or the story of Shane McConkey, one of the great downhill skiers who decided skiing down a mountain that can only be accessed by helicopter wasn't enough, that maybe parachuting off of the mountain with his skis on was a better way to end the run. And there is the story of Laird Hamilton who helped to invent "tow-in" surfing on waves so big that the only way to ride them is to be pulled by jet skis to get enough speed to catch a wave sixty to a hundred feet high. The book seeks to understand how these athletes accomplish these seemingly impossible feats. What is it that helps them to survive these very extreme situations? Flow is the answer. Flow is described in the book as an optimal state of consciousness, a peak state where we both feel at our best and perform our best. Through the stories of these superhumans we are introduced to the science of flow and the mindset of these incredible pioneers. The book introduces us to extreme kayakers, mountain climbers, base jumpers and more as we learn what lessons flow has for us. It is my first book on flow, but not my last. This book was fun to read, as the characters were brought to life by the author with full context of the mindset of the extreme athletes. Bookshelf material.

How to Fail at Almost Everything and Still Win Big, **Scott Adams (Portfolio, 2013).** Scott Adams is the creator of the *Dilbert* comic strip and author of multiple books. He has recently received a lot of attention for accurately predicting Donald Trump's victory in the presidential election. A part of his expertise is in persuasion as a trained hypnotist. The premise of the book is that you need to take action and not be afraid to fail. In fact, he argues, failure is a key ingredient to growth, as the training and lessons learned while solving problems provide useful in later endeavors. The reason I love this book is because it is so practical. The book tells Scott's story as he moved from New York state to Northern California following in his brothers' footsteps to pursue his dreams. You follow Scott from one failure to another and along the way pick up some great tips and tricks to success. The primary and most eye opening for me was the idea that "goals are for losers." This is the exact opposite of what I have been taught my entire sales career. Instead of goals, Adams says systems are the key to success. For instance, you might have a goal to lose forty pounds this year. He would encourage you to get closer to that ideal in a more realistic way, by setting up systems that contribute to that outcome. Other really big ideas in this book are: 1) What you put into your mind also comes back out—in other words, garbage in garbage out—so be careful what you feed your mind; 2) Only measure one metric, your personal energy. This personal energy is the building block to productivity and happiness in your life; 3) Skills are more important than talent. Learning a skill that combines with other skills or talents you already have will make you more valuable to potential employers or business partners. I love this book and refer to it regularly.

***The Power of Right Believing,* Joseph Prince (FaithWords, 2013).**
Ok, I don't want to come off as a religious zealot. Actually, I am NOT religious, AT ALL. However, I love Jesus. More importantly, He loves me. I believe relationship is way more important than religion. Men, through the centuries, have hijacked the message of Jesus Christ and have perverted it for their own gain. This book is revolutionary. If you grew up in church and you hate church, please buy this book. You will be introduced to a Jesus you never knew existed. A Jesus who has got your back. Someone who is more concerned about you as a person and not a "performer." Performance-based relationships are poison. If you've ever read the stories about the "stage moms" or "soccer dads" who live their dreams through their children and force them to perform, you know how badly those stories end. So it is with God. He is not about the rules, he is all about the relationship. I did not know this for most of my life, but now that I do, my life has been transformed. This book introduces the importance of believing the "right" things about Christ. Do we live by the "law" or by "grace."? Prince tells the story of how for more than 1,500 years there were no Ten Commandments, no law. He shows how men, over time, have tried to live life by "keeping the law" (performing), and just how futile and destructive this behavior is. He introduces grace that unleashes our relationship with God because we operate with the promise that Jesus Christ died once, for all sins past and future. Settled. Paid for. Now rest. Relax. Enjoy the relationship, enjoy the journey, worship God from a position of being forgiven un-conditionally, from a place of freedom. I listen to his podcast almost every morning to help get my mind right. I love this message and this book. For those who worry about apostasy, he backs everything with scripture—it's all biblically based.

***Tribes, We Need You to Lead Us,* Seth Godin (Portfolio, 2008).**
In addition to being one of my favorite writers, Godin is a modern

marketing genius. More than that, he's become a source of wisdom for me on a more important topic, human connection. Seth doesn't watch television. He says that gives him seven more hours per day than most other people. It gives him time to read, which in turn gives him wisdom, especially when it comes to reaching out to people. Inbound marketing is what many in the business call it. In *Tribes,* Godin makes the point that there are people out there who are looking for a leader. You, as a business person or leader within your organization, need to step up and lead them. But it's not what you think. You must first put your leadership on display via media and attract your audience. YouTube, blogging, newsletters, social media—all are ways to engage your audience and, through your encouragement, connect the group, your tribe. There's incredible insight and wisdom in the chapter called *The Plurality Myth.* Godin introduces the fallacy of the plurality. You don't need 51 percent of the audience to agree with you. Instead, lead your very distinct and exclusive tribe, the one that most reflects your views and passion. The book can be summed up here: "Trying to lead everyone results in leading no one in particular." The beauty is, "you get to choose the tribe you will lead."

The 4-Hour Workweek, Timothy Ferris (Edbury Press, 2011). A friend introduced me to Tim Ferris's podcast a couple of years ago. Until then I didn't know what a podcast was, much less who Tim Ferris was. There are five podcasts I listen to religiously and Ferris is number one. (The others are Ryan Fletcher, James Altucher, Joe Rogan and Joseph Prince for spiritual enrichment.) Ferris is a human experiment machine. This book, along with his new book *Tools of Titans,* should be on your bookshelf side by side. In the *4-Hour Workweek,* he shows you a new way to think. He is continually testing concepts and putting them into practice. Many are in this book. Memorable lessons include: The Pareto Principle which states that 80 percent of your results come from 20 percent of your efforts. Said another way: Focus on the 20 percent if you want massive increases in productivity and results. He introduces the concept of efficient vs. effective, and how the Pareto Principle homes in on what is effective. Parkinson's Principle is another concept everyone should know. The idea is that if you have two weeks to do a project, it will take two weeks. However, if you decide that you have one week, it can be done in one week. It's mindset: Your project will fill up whatever amount of time you dedicate to it, so why not create a new paradigm and finish sooner? In Chapter 6, you are introduced to the low-information diet. The author confesses that he never watches the news, and almost never reads a newspaper. Keeping ignorant about selected information and interruptions that are irrelevant, unimportant, or unactionable, is vital to a successful life. "There are many things of which a wise man might wish to be ignorant," said Ralph Waldo Emerson. This book offers so many principles and lessons and new ways to think and operate, with practical tips on how to handle our day to day life. Don't miss this book.

ACKNOWLEDGMENTS

—ɯ—

Ryan Fletcher: Without you I would not have had the audacity to think I could write a book.

Doug Feagles: Thank you for all of our time spent together and showing me the way of the Jedi.

To my writing coach and editor Pete Bronson: Thanks so much for the encouragement and wisdom, and for patiently listening to the madness.

To my kids, Scott and Krista Adams: Thanks for inspiring me. Every day I write, I write for you.

And to all the others—friends, family and business associates—who have inspired me and encouraged me: Thank you.

bas·tion: an institution, place, or person strongly defending or upholding particular principles, attitudes, or activities. *Synonyms*: stronghold, bulwark, defender, support, guard, protection, protector, defender.

If you would like to learn more about joining Bastion REALTORS® or would just like more info regarding storytelling, please email Ron direct at ron@bastionrealtors.com.

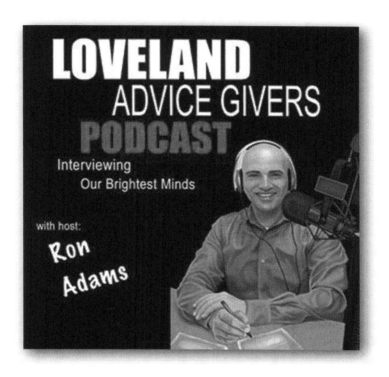

Check out my podcast on iTunes and Stitcher.com to learn more about storytelling and relationships. You can also listen directly at my website: www.LovelandAdviceGivers.com.

ABOUT THE AUTHOR

—ɯ—

RON ADAMS IS SUPERMAN...

Wait, let's try that again.

Ron Adams is the founder of Bastion REALTORS® located in Loveland, Ohio. He and his wife, Theresa, live in Loveland with their two dogs, Austin and Dez. Ron is the host of the podcast *Loveland Advice Givers;* the editor in chief of *Advisor Monthly Magazine;* and the host of the YouTube show *Bastion Daily.*

Reading comic books at the age of 8, he decided he wanted to grow up to be Superman. He also came across an advertisement that encouraged him to start a business selling seeds door to door. He's been an entrepreneur ever since—which is good, because the Superman thing did not work out.

Most of his career was in sales and sales management for building materials, while simultaneously coaching and following his two children, Scott and Krista, all over the country on soccer fields, basketball courts, and music venues.

After the graduation of his daughter from college and with both kids out of the house, he wondered what every comic book fan has asked: "What happens next?" This question led him down a winding road of self-discovery. The culmination of that journey is this book.

Geared for business professionals, **"Salesperson to Superhero"** explores how to live a life of significance by seeking meaning in work. It's not going to unleash gamma rays that turn you into the Incredible Hulk, but it could change your life and your business.

If you want to find your purpose, tell your story, and execute your mission, this book is your roadmap to professional and personal success. It shows the way to develop relationships through storytelling.

"I want everyone to be successful by finding their talents and passion," Adams says. "There's a Superman or Wonder Woman in each of us. Everyone has a story to tell. Yours could change your world."

Made in the USA
Columbia, SC
30 January 2018